INSPIRATION FROM THE INNER "I"

INSPIRATION
FROM THE INNER

Norman V. Olsson

CSA Press *Publisher*
Lakemont, Georgia 30552

Standard Book Number 0-87707-218-3

To contact the author write him directly at:
6226 Charlottesville, San Antonio, Texas 78233

Manufactured in the United States of America

Dedicated to my Wife

HELEN

*divine companion, honest critic,
helpmate in momentous matters
and little details, sharing as
love requires with a joy that
softens my more serious nature.*

ABOUT THE AUTHOR

Leaving a successful business career, Norman Olsson was still a young executive when he entered the ministerial training at Unity School of Christianity. After graduation he spent nine weeks in the Northwest as a supply minister and was then assigned the leadership of Church of Unity, Cleveland, Ohio. He was ordained in 1960. Under his spiritual administration, the church developed from rented quarters to an active ministry in the west surburban area of the city. He was responsible for its growth and prosperity from a ministry that had no tangible property value. Three acres of land were purchased and finally a new construction was completed in Westlake, Ohio in April, 1971. He then took a much needed sabbatical from the field ministry.

In 1973 he accepted the leadership of Unity Church of San Antonio. There, as in Cleveland, he reorganized the church and developed a full ministerial program. Also, as before, permanent property was acquired to end many years of uncertain rental conditions. He continues as the minister of Unity Church of San Antonio at this present time.

Before he entered the ministry, Norman Olsson had begun a free lance writing career. He has had more than 50 articles and poems published the past twenty-two years.

The major portion of his writings have appeared in Unity publications, often being featured several times a year. In his dedication to the Unity movement as a writer, he has literally provided inspiration to millions of readers. Through his unique administrative talent and business background, a permanent church home for Unity followers in two major cities of the United States has been secured.

The author is a provocative spiritual teacher, well-grounded in his metaphysical concepts. His articles are originally instructive and the poetic side of his nature expresses in the meditations of this book as well as in his poetry. For this, his first published book, he has written new material to accompany the content of previously published writings. The anthology of material has been arranged so the reader can easily select a subject, reading for short periods of inspiration or for more in-depth study. Happy reading!

CONTENTS

PREFACE

Spiritual growth is an identification process as the self-conscious you comes to recognize the Divine "I." In the absolute realm the One Power and One Presence declares, as was revealed to Moses, "I AM WHO I AM." We, who are the individuated spirits of God, cannot fully comprehend the Absolute One through personal awareness. In our more enlightened states of consciousness we do know as did John, "He who is in you is greater than he who is in the world."

The master key to unlock the doors of inner perception, open all the inner faculties, is spiritual insight. My book is devoted to the encouragement of insight in others, through meditation, through recognizing insight in itself, and through developing the "divine knack" of letting insights happen. There is a creative process that no teaching or religion can ever systematize or formalize, which is why the best creed cannot guarantee answered prayer. "For the foolishness of God is wiser than men, and the weakness of God is stronger than men."

My religion honors all truths as reflections of the One Truth. I believe pure intuition, "the eye of the soul," makes possible our seeing the Life of our life, the Mind of our mind, the Love of our love—the One Self within many selves. God is identified within us all as the Divine "I." Every authentic mystic, every illumined metaphysician,

11

every real minister knows the yoga of the East and the West recommends union of self with God, the attainment of Christhood as Christians name it.

You, for your part, can find self-realization and supreme fulfillment by letting the Divine "I" become what It chooses to be. You experience divine unfoldment of the Divine "I" in you and through you as transcendent states of consciousness. Always be mindful, however, that the glorification of God will not be distracted by personal gains unsuited to Its own end. You can literally accept what Jesus taught: "He who loses his life for my sake will find it." The great paradox of life is that a higher gain requires a lesser loss. An ancient teacher of Tao expressed what is called "Letting go and letting God" in this very profound yet simply stated poetic form of wisdom:

> The student learns by daily increment.
> The Way is gained by daily loss,
> Loss upon loss until
> At last comes rest.
>
> By letting go, it all gets done;
> The world is won by those who let it go!
> But when you try and try,
> The world is then beyond the winning.

A lot of activity on the human treadmill is no more productive than it is for a mouse in a research laboratory. "All is vanity" applies to unillumined human effort. Even so, there is a grand and divine purpose behind our being in this preparatory phase of becoming. Wherever you are at this time, whatever the circumstances of your life, learn to enjoy the commonplace and appreciate the creative plot behind the human story as it appears. The stage is set for gods in the making. Meditating for pure motivation you realize you are never alone. Your Divine "I" indwells you as the Lord of your being. Listen for every subtle cue from the One who is Author of it all. Develop insight. It is the ear of the heart!

THE QUIET WAY
WILL OVERCOME

I let the Spirit come into my inner life as silently as the day dawns. Just as a flower is shaped to the perfection of its own nature, I will to be shaped from within my heart center. I trust the quiet way of unfoldment.

Now I free myself from feeling burdened by worldly ties. I put aside the personal will and ego mind. I rest in the knowing that I am the inheritor of a divine nature. No human striving will be allowed to keep me from attaining my inner peace in unity with God. I let go my lesser nature, forgive all and everyone, surrender my very soul, and listen for that "still small voice" within.

In my quiet way I wait, wait with a feeling of detachment, a sense of timelessness. I prepare myself to receive the many blessings God wishes to bestow upon me. I reach that exalted state of expectancy that sees the open doors of unlimited good.

A gentle transformation keeps lifting me up to new heights of consciousness. The light of spiritual illumination begins its dawning in my soul. Christ within never fails to resurrect me in my time of need for renewal. Whatever I must face in the world, I know the quiet way will overcome!

"Be still, and know that I am God."

INSIGHTS FROM THE DIVINE "I"

How does one become a spiritually illumined soul? The question relates directly to the ultimate goal for one's self-fulfillment and overshadows all other human objectives and personal achievement. It can only be answered in the context that we are all going through a divine process. The process is the continual awakening of the soul to its true nature in God. Though a person in the human states of awareness may seldom identify with God, the Divine "I" maintains an eternal vigil and ultimately will not be denied. "If you will not awake, I will come like a thief, and you will not know at what hour I will come upon you." (Revelation 3:3)

There is a continual influx of God activity, traditionally called the movement of the Holy (Whole) Spirit, that makes possible divine insights. Many insights come when we least expect and through the years we all receive our share of personal insights, simply because "The light shines in the darkness, and the darkness has not overcome it." Greater insights are known today as spiritual breakthroughs. They come through everyday experiences or in seemingly supernatural encounters that cannot be rationally explained. True spiritual insight is a perception of the inner nature and real character of self and life, seeing the reality of Being that endures. Paul said, "For now we see in a mirror dimly, but then face to face." Seeing dimly excites illusions, indulgence in the magic of mind imagery,

14

and often confuses psychic phenomena with true insight. "Face to face" is when the virtue of the Divine "I" is glimpsed by the soul and the essence of that high moment flourishes forever in one's consciousness. So "the perishable puts on the imperishable, and the mortal puts on immortality" insight upon insight till the soul is fully awakened.

Inner inspiration changes the consciousness, uplifting the soul on its spiral path to heavenly heights. There are both motivational books and inspirational literature being printed today in unprecedented volume. The world hungers and thirsts for righteousness as never before. Many people need to be motivated to a course of action, as when a sales person convinces a customer or client to buy a certain product or service. That is at the "doing level" of life. Then there is the learning of mind methods and techniques to activate the inner faculties through a mental approach to more positive and constructive expression of the whole person. That is associated with the "personal knowing level." The highest path simply recommends that we learn "to be." This path is not exclusively Christian, but is the foundation principle of the mystical life found in the metaphysics of all great spiritual teachings. The Divine "I" has long been known as "The true light that enlightens every man." The Hindu, having his own name for the Christ, looks to the Atman, Supreme Soul of the universe, for spiritual insight. The Buddhist seeks to attain Bodhisattva, the perfect illumination that demonstrates the living Buddha. Insights from the Divine "I" have brought and continue to bring revelation and enlightenment throughout every culture, civilization and age to produce great spiritual teachers, saints, and self-realized souls. Whatever exalted name is given to the Divine "I," It is always with us in our forever becomingness. It extricates us with a saving grace from our deep involvement with growth phases and teaches us "to be." Who and what we are "to be" is learned insight upon insight until we literally "overcome the world."

The message of this book is to inspire the reader on the path of the divine process to become a fully awakened soul. It shares my insights from the Divine "I." Many of these insights you will readily identify with in your own life. Some, I trust, will inspire you to find new insights for yourself. No one can force an insight. They "come like a thief" when you may least expect. Truth is like penetrating oil and will reach the most rusty states of minds when our human guard is down. But we can initiate spiritual insight. The best way is through meditative practices, about which more will be said. Nothing is gained without a sustained conscious effort and higher desire "to be."

Although I am a minister in the field of Christian metaphysics, my dedication goes beyond one religion, a particular school of thought, or an organized viewpoint. I have received insights from the Divine "I" throughout my ministerial career of twenty-two years, and before. Many of these insights have provided the inspiration for numerous articles and poems continuously published through the latter period of my life. Much of my writing has appeared in Unity periodicals, some in Science of Mind magazine and the Truth Journal. Full credit is gratefully given in the bibliography of this edition for my having reprint rights. The articles and poems have been classified along with other material into special sections of the book. This is for the reader's convenience to provide quick reference by subject for selective reading.

Some years ago a provocative and easily remembered mini-instruction came to my attention through a metaphysical teacher. It states: "It is good to know. It is better to do. It is best to be." The latter refers to the letting go of the ego-centered self and letting the Divine "I" illumine the soul to see and claim its true divine nature. On this plane we must increase our knowing, meet our responsibilities of what may often seem to be endless doing. Even so, the most important challenge is to be what we were created to be. We can help ourselves along on the spiritual path by working with and developing insights from the

Divine "I." All we need to be spiritually illumined souls is
within, where the Divine "I" maintains an eternal vigil to
come unto Its own. Why not now?

MEDITATING FOR PURE MOTIVATION

It is not enough to meditate only for relaxation, momentary peace of mind, inner refuge from the world. All these goals serve a purpose for what might be called conditioning your consciousness. Although your destiny is to be perfected and extends through infinite dimensions about which we gain "intimations of immortality," this immediate temporal life is focused on a plane of reality where organic and spiritual growth are fused together. In our becomingness there is outer work to be done in a synchronized correspondence with the awakening of the individual soul. A spiritual motivation must be established for one to fill his or her rightful role in the "here and now." A consciousness of success is needed in the living out of our relationship with loved ones, others, friends, society, the whole race and its evolution. This phase of our being in the divine process is vital to our future.

As a higher consciousness is attained the dedication to human reponsibilities must not lessen. Mahatma Gandhi spent a portion of his day at the spinning wheel and called his labor a "sacrament" that turned his mind "Godward." Jesus was so dedicated in his healing ministry he worked on the sabbath and was then confronted by authorities for having broken the Judaic law. His very explicit reply to them was "My Father is working still, and I am working."

As great teachers and saints rise above personal will and renounce human striving, they gain in return a motivational spirit that works tirelessly and impersonally for the good of all.

Does it seem strange to you that this inner posture of passivity, which is found in meditation, must not be allowed to trap you into tight little pockets of tranquillity? There is always the temptation to use detachment as an escape from outer challenges on the human scene of involvement. On one occasion Jesus invited his disciples to take a sabbatical from their devoted service to his ministry. He said, "Come away by yourselves to a lonely place, and rest a while." The key phrase in this instruction is "rest a while." No one can be effective in any type of work or profession without taking time for spiritual infilling. Both ministers and businessmen alike often overlook the continual need for self-renewal. So frequency of meditation is more important than letting it be a long indulgence to shut out the world as something evil.

In going apart to meditate we enter into a state of timeless consciousness called "The Silence." The Silence is Reality untouched by worldly limitation and each time we go apart we can give thanks if we gain just one insight from the Divine "I" that abides there. Each insight brings with it a new awakening for the soul. In time, as we identify with the Divine "I," also known as Christ within, we reach a place of conscious growth when there is a new or second birth. Our human birth is like an ordinary seed and contains in it the same tenacious growth impulse once it germinates. The seed of a wild grass will, for example, penetrate a crack in a super highway or grow in the dust the crevice of a building may provide many feet above ground. Organic life will not be deterred from becoming what it was created to be once its dormant life is rooted and awakened. In the new or second birth, the seed of Christ roots in human consciousness and often leaves the outer ego self in turmoil and confusion until it surrenders. Paul recognized this and said it was a matter of him dying daily in the process. When he found his spiritual maturity, he announced with a tone of triumph. "It is no longer I who live, but Christ who lives in me." So the spiritual life becomes established by transforming the organic and tenacious life to Its own end.

Trust meditation to make your transformation through a new or second birth a wonderful metamorphosis you can consciously enjoy and experience with the wonder of being. "Born again Christians" in the traditional and fundamental experience get a sensual and psychic rapture that still has to be worked out and refined in consciousness to make the soul fertile for the Christ seed. Even so, by some instinct or extreme inner longing, they get to the threshold and know there is a door that opens to personal salvation. It is like someone being in the vestibule and believing he is spiritually at home. But the divine process is not completed by any shortcut. It is a divine growth that brings unfoldment insight after insight. We receive the seed of Christ and it must bloom in the consciousness. Jesus explained this in a parable. "The kingdom of God is as if a man should scatter seed upon the ground, and should sleep and rise night and day, and the seed should sprout and grow, he knows not how. The earth produces of itself, first the blade, then the ear, and then the full grain in the ear." (Mark 4:26-28) The tenacious seed of organic life will not be thwarted once it takes root. Likewise, when the seed of Christ germinates in your awakening soul, the Word proceeds to be made flesh. To recognize the Christ seed, which in itself is gaining a supreme insight from the Divine "I," is to find a "pearl of great value" for which you would literally make any sacrifice. I use the term sacrifice in the sense that you would know how to give up the lesser for the greater without feeling any loss.

Try to think of meditation as more than one form or practice. Consider it, quite simply, as an inner going apart to submit yourself to the Divine "I." This submission is for spiritual insight. Insight upon insight reveals the divine identity within you, awakens the soul, brings the Christ seed to bloom. This divine process promises you a beautiful journey through life, the continual emergence of Christ in you as you merge yourself in Christ. As Gertrude Stein said, "a rose is a rose is a rose." So we Westerners must respect the Hindu, the Buddhist, the Taoist, every believer for whatever way they follow in recognizing the rose of self.

The meditative experience can happen anywhere, at any time. It must bring insight and spiritual motivation. Just let it happen! A pause and delay on the golf course, a reflective moment while fishing, deeper contemplation in the course of one's common activities, even waiting in your car for a traffic jam to clear, all provide a perfect setting for an insight that can change both your life and your consciousness. If you find you get good results from yoga, a spiritual teacher, a special method, all well and good. Be mindful, however, that an insight cannot be programmed, forced, or guaranteed by a highly rated technique. Insights come in divinely natural ways. God truly is no respecter of person. No one has a privileged status in gaining access to the One Reality. We should go within with the innocence of a little child. As we develop an awareness of this divine process we learn how to work with it, cooperate with the Divine "I." One soon realizes there is a "divine knack" to meditation and it proves to happen more and more because you desire to be awakened, so become inclined to submit yourself to be what you were created to be.

The reader will find various meditations associated with the topical themes presented in the book. It is my belief the quiet reading of each in a contemplative mood may prove to excite new states of consciousness. The written word can be divinely suggestive, but only the Spirit can work the miracle of a new insight. May it happen to you!

I
INSIGHTS FROM SCRIPTURAL CONTEMPLATION

THE METAPHYSICAL TRINITY

"God in three phases, not three persons apart or outside you, exists in you, and you in God. Every thought you and I think is linked to the universality of our being and the atomic energies that constitute the life forces."

There is an old Christian hymn, the refrain of which includes the phrase, "God in three persons, blessed trinity." How can this be possible? It is still believed literally by many people. But three cannot be one, and the theological implications cannot really be understood except in metaphysical terms. There is a metaphysical trinity. It has a very profound and beautiful meaning for us, and can be explained with no intent to discredit the substance of its truth as conceived centuries ago.

It all began when the Nicene Council was held in A.D. 325, during the time of the Roman emperor Constantine. To stabilize the rival pagan and early Christian factions of his regime, he saw it expedient to work out a doctrinal belief that would carry religious weight and be politically compromising. The personal profile of divinity was quite acceptable as a general concept in that time, whether one worshiped God or gods. The trinity nature was upheld as sacred and stated as "Father, son, and holy ghost (holy spirit)." It caught a glimpse of the divine nature without the whole realization, and given the seal of infallible decree, it still survives as a tenet of faith today.

God as Father is the Source of all, Divine Mind, absolute Being. The Son is the divine idea of individuated Spirit, the Christ, the ideal Self. The Holy Spirit defines the whole activity of God expressed throughout creation. Metaphysically speaking, there are three phases of God rather than three faces. To conceive of God as a multiple deity is confusing and unnecessarily mystifying. There is a verse in Ecclesiastes that states, "A threefold cord is not quickly broken." So we should regard the trinity as one cord of unbroken reality. Put in more understandable terms, the trinity in its known and observable reality is Mind-idea-expression. That may not sound theological, but it can be more readily related to the phenomena of life everywhere.

One thing is certain: Jesus never implied that there are three divine persons. Nowhere in the Scriptures can one find the word *trinity* or such a doctrine. Jesus always spoke of divine unity and stressed personal unification within the Spirit: "I am in my Father, and you in me, and I in you." He implied that there were phases of identity, and his teachings portrayed the human part as the shadow of the divine light ("let your light so shine").

The trinity in its phases can be identified in the study of mind and consciousness. There is the supermind, the subconscious mind, and the conscious mind. The superconsciousness refers to Christ awareness. Subconsciousness is the heart, feeling nature, seat of memory, subjective nature, and computer faculty of mind. The conscious mind includes one's state of personal awareness, ego, self-consciousness. The equation of three phases in what we call life and being keeps repeating. As a creation one is spirit-soul-body. Living things have substance, life, and intelligence to some degree. Every atom has substance (an element), life (energy), and intelligence (a directed action).

Walt Whitman, who caught the cosmic nature of the individual in his universalism of thought, said, "Man's not all included between his hat and his boots." Each person has a trinity of being, three phases in one rather than three persons in one. If we trace the thread of the human person to the creative beginning, there is one divine person, or Supreme Being. God gives us identity and we can return the gift by being the best spiritual person possible. This is accomplished by unifying the three phases of our being.

The highest phase of being was constantly called "Lord" in the Old Testament. Lord means guardian, a person or power, keeper of the law. Your indwelling Lord is the law of your being, the highest identity of self which is inviolable, supreme, eternal, pure. In the soul we see the other two phases, conscious mind (head) and subconscious mind (heart). These two phases are always interacting upon each other. Because so many people live in a duality of self-expression, head and heart at odds, uncoordinated and not unified to the Lord of being, the professional field for counselors, psychiatrists, and psychologists keeps expanding. More "do-it-yourself" treatment can succeed by taking seriously the oft-quoted and ageless admonition "Know thyself." Know yourself as a trinity. Get the right profile of God and you can get a truer picture of yourself.

A little girl was out walking one starry night with her father. She seemed so absorbed with the magnificence of the sky overhead that he asked what she was thinking. "Oh," she replied, "I was thinking, Daddy, that if the wrong side of heaven is so glorious, what must the right side be!" So it is with our understanding of ancient concepts. The theological trinity does allude to the truth, but it misrepresents the true nature of God and no longer satisfies the searching mind of today. It is too cryptic and pontifical. It is the wrong side of reality, and metaphysical teachings today are revealing the right side, the metaphysical trinity.

When we say "I am," asserting our spiritual nature, we speak from the higher phase of self as the divine person. The soul draws power from this first or cause phase of being into itself, into consciousness and realization, and then distributes the energy, virtue, quality it recognizes to the outer expression.

From the personal point of view, which is our immediate point of reference, demonstration is initiated at the conscious mind level. From the Christ self or superconscious mind we can call forth the spiritual idea, ideal, and literally speak it into action. The Word is the source and using the power of the Word, either audibly or through formative thought, is the way to bring our good into manifestation. If one speaks only out of the personal subconscious level, subjectivity of the outer self, it can be either good, bad, or indifferent, depending upon what is being expressed or reactively touched within. Only in the Christ consciousness can one speak with what can be called spiritual authority. We do have to monitor ourself, be aware of what phase of mind or consciousness we are expressing from.

A farmer's wife who was very popular was asked her secret for making and keeping so many friends. "There's no secret to it," she explained. "I'm just careful to taste my words real good before I let them get past my teeth." To avoid what might be the unpleasantness (as the cliché puts it) of "eating our words," we do well to taste them before endowing them with power. Jesus spoke out of His Christ consciousness when He said, "The words that I have spoken to you are spirit and life." Our triune nature offers us the opportunity at all times to express the supreme Self.

You are a trinity. You are a person with three phases of being. The purpose of faith and love is to use the power of believing and unite all phases into a fulfilled expression of individuality. This requires integrating the spiritual, emotional, and intellectual nature as one. God in three phases, not three persons apart or outside you, exists in you, and you in God. Every thought you and I think is linked to the universality of our being and the atomic energies that constitute the life forces. Taking conscious thought is the initial step that can unite all phases of being, bring the total consciousness into that consummate expression we often call fulfillment. Emerson said, "Thought must take the stupendous step of passing into realization."

Perhaps the theological trinity provided a beginning for the unenlightened masses of the fourth century. Now we live in the atomic age, not in the horse-and-chariot culture of those days when the Council of Nicene was held. The spirit of new thought and metaphysical understanding, perceiving more deeply the message of Jesus Christ and the true meaning of the Bible, penetrates the mystery of three persons to help each of us see ourself as a divine person. It is our divine right to say, "Father, glorify thou me in thy own presence with the glory which I had with thee before the world was made."

THE GOSPEL TRUTH

A few yesterdays ago it was often said, to support one's veracity in making any kind of testimony, "It's the gospel truth!" This implies an ingrained belief in the letter that exceeds the spirit in itself, although such a statement usually expresses a reverence for the authority of Matthew, Mark, Luke, and John. It also reflects traditional fundamentalism that persists in our colloquial relations.

The Gospel writers told about Jesus from each one's individual viewpoint, as well as recording what the Master taught. There is a distinction between what the writer reports personally and what he records as an exact quotation. In today's world, newspapers report and editorialize. But reading what a celebrity or leader actually said is usually more nearly accurate. Sooner or later, one must decide, in his Truth study, "What is the chaff to the wheat?" Is the mythological and supernatural accounting of Jesus' birth beyond question? Is it the gospel truth?

My own background was one of very thorough indoctrination. I was raised in a traditional Sunday school, spent portions of my carefree summers in vacation Bible school, and was properly confirmed. I am grateful for this background. Throughout my teens and early manhood I read the Gospels and studied them in the freer privacy of my own consciousness, needing no prompting. Today, I still hold the teachings of Jesus to be the gospel of the Christ Spirit speaking forth to mankind. Singular verses deepen for me in their spiritual majesty and meaning as time passes by.

It saddens me when someone seeking counsel has let any shadow of doubt cast upon Jesus' birth (the Nativity story in particular) cause a religious trauma. Over the years I have encountered many sincere Christians who worry too much about the authenticity of the Gospel reporting and editorializing, as though this could change the Beatitudes, the Sermon on the Mount, the precepts and example of Jesus Christ.

I believe that the Synoptic Gospels carried a common viewpoint written for their time, which John carefully avoided in considering posterity. Have you ever wondered why John, the most intimate disciple of Jesus, makes no reference that can be considered mythological? He does not report a supernatural birth. He simply states that the divine spark blazed into the spiritual manifestation of a man. "In the beginning was the Word . . . and the Word became flesh." Nor does he set Jesus apart from other men. "The true light that enlightens every man was coming into the world." That is the Nativity story for modern man.

One should not feel a disillusionment over the question of what is the mythological and who was the real Son of God. As Jesus once said, "Let not your hearts be troubled." He referred to Himself by His spiritual identity in saying, "I am the way, the truth, and the life." We find this verse in John's Gospel. Jesus makes no self-reference that can be termed mythological or supernatural with respect to His birth. Genealogy neither adds to nor subtracts from one's spiritual stature. Whether we all once were hanging from the same family tree or share Adam and Eve as a common parental beginning, is it not enough to believe with John, "If you abide in me, and my words abide in you, ask whatever you will, and it shall be done for you"?

The Christ teaching is all. The birth of Jesus does not change the message of Truth, no matter what the historical truth may be about the event.

Research and study convince me that the Synoptic Gospel writers—Matthew, Mark, and Luke—"told a story" when they told the Nativity tale. They did this, I believe, because their readers were almost all superstitious and mostly of pagan ancestry. Remember, the Gospels were written in the first century A.D. No one then believed in a savior or a spiritual image of worship who did not appear on earth in a supernatural way. Virgin-birth mythology is part of most great religions, and predates our Christian account. It was a common legend of pagan cults. The more sophisticated Greek believed his gods to be superhuman, bred in supernatural ways. There was an acceptance of what is now called theogony, meaning that a god was sired when the gods descended to select a woman as the one divinely blessed. The belief was held in ancient Egypt. Julius Caesar was supposed to have been conceived by his mother in the temple of Apollo. So Matthew, Mark, and Luke gave Jesus the credentials most needed to insure public acceptance of Him as a Savior, the Messiah. They wanted to avoid a credibility gap! They did not anticipate the traumatic confusion they were creating for a later age. Only John avoided taking "author's license." The Gospel according to John lets Jesus' teachings stand on their own merit, and gives the metaphysical viewpoint.

Think back over relatively recent history, how royal families are diminishing because the world has finally rejected the notion of birth by divine right. Of course we can symbolize the myth, interpret the legend, find deeper truths, and give them spiritual meaning. Interpreting what each symbol and supernatural event portends requires extensive metaphysical study in itself. But the "simply profound and profoundly simple" truths in the Jesus Christ teachings far transcend any controversy over His origin or birth. He was more concerned with man's new birth, with being "born anew . . . of the Spirit." (This teaching to Nicodemus was recorded by John.)

Buddha, the savior type of another race, another age, before the time of Jesus, cautioned his disciples, "There is another great prohibition which I proclaim to you: an ordained disciple must not boast of any superhuman perfection." He knew of the natural inclination on the part of disciples to magnify their leader. This has been done in our day, because the phenomenon of man's believing nature knows no bounds (which is good if the yeast of imagination does not run wild).

This is my viewpoint, not intended to challenge your peace of mind or to change any of your beliefs. I hope that it will give you either a new realization or a deeper sense of believing that exalts what the Teacher taught, rather than what His disciples said about Him. Contemporary thinking is changing with regard to the Nativity story, but the Jesus Christ truths become more powerful in being questioned. As Jesus said, "Heaven and earth will pass away, but my words will not pass away."

As a metaphysical teacher, I believe that John is the best and foremost authority on Jesus Christ in reporting His origin and recording His message. John kept a record of living words overlooked by the other Gospel writers. He wrote for us, the new age. But you must determine for yourself where the literal and spiritual divide, what is the wheat and what is the chaff. When you question anything, you do it by the power of the Spirit that frees you to transcend your birth, your background, and adjust your spiritual eyes to the Light that lights all men. By all means, question until you are satisfied. Ask yourself, "Is it the gospel truth?"

GOD REFLECTED IN A SPARROW'S EYE

For many years the gospel verse that testifies a sparrow "shall [not] fall on the ground without your Father" would come to my attention through some phase of my ministerial activity, often in my reading.

The verse was commonly understood by me, and I believe by most of us, to mean that the least form of life could not die in this world without the omniscient awareness of God. The verse circulated in my memory because its profound meaning was beyond any superficial interpretation. Then, one cold November morning, two years ago, I was literally to experience what is the truth of this teaching in itself.

My experience began that day as I went to the glass sliding doors that open to our patio. I was in my robe, because it was my morning habit to look out over the open field and trees in the background beyond our property. It is an inspiring and enchanting moment to greet the freshness of a new day, especially when the oblique rays of the sun alight everywhere with a soft touch.

Having had my fill of the scene, I was about to back away and go to the breakfast table when I spied the stiff figure of a small sparrow on the concerete below the door-sill. The poor thing had no doubt flown into the glass door, unaware of the barrier to its flight.

33

An impulse, which at first was curiosity, led me to pick up this seemingly lifeless form. In the palm of my hand its feathery form felt cold, completely inert. I was tempted to dispose of it in a humane way, but instinctively I held out hope for revival.

My wife suggested applying a drop of water to the sparrow's beak, so I went to the faucet and let a drop or two settle on my finger. The warmth of my hand and the wet touch of the water together must have had a miraculous effect. I sensed a response and stroked the crown of its head very gently, all the time encouraging my diminutive patient with the words "There, that's a good little bird!"

Never had I, having picked up a few dead birds in the past, witnessed one recover from such a rigid, death-like condition. The second time I touched water to its beak it seemed to drink very feebly.

For about thirty seconds, it lay semiconscious in my hand, and then it lifted up its head in a majestic gesture and looked deeply into my attentive eyes. We had perfect eye contact. Indescribable as it was, I must try to explain what did actually happen. The sparrow and I seemed to be portals through which the very Spirit of God was consciously reflected between us. It seemed as though we were aware of this as we were locked in one gaze. We understood each other as having no lesser or greater significance in our creative relationship.

A wave of compassion engulfed me, and I knew I was not the benefactor, but a witness to a portion of the Father's life transcending its outer expression in return to its divine source. The momentary passing of this frail and minute being renewed my faith, confirmed my belief in immortality, and revealed the unity of all life. It was nothing less than a sign from heaven.

One never knows how simply, sweetly, and suddenly spiritual reality can be unveiled. I had found a fallen sparrow that I thought would be uneventfully returned to the elements, only an incident to delay my breakfast slightly. Instead of such a mundane distraction, I was truly privileged to see God reflected in a sparrow's eye. And I am equally sure a sparrow saw God reflected in a human's eye.

It brought to my mind, afterward, that I had experienced the deeper truth of two gospel teachings. The first truth had to do with a sparrow's not falling to the ground without the Father's knowledge. The second truth, which I later recalled over and over again, was Jesus' statement, "Inasmuch as ye have done *it* unto one of the least of these my brethren, ye have done *it* unto me."

This experience gave me one of the most precious moments in my life. It could have been a very commonplace happening had it not been for the inner recognition, the loving oneness that transpired between two creatures whose lives seldom relate to each other in a mutual fulfillment. Seeing God reflected in the eye of a sparrow, or in another human being, is surely an act of grace, a miracle that I trust will someday be perceived among men and all creatures in the interrelation of their lives—"seeing he himself giveth to all life, and breath, and all things."

THE MIND LOCK

The subconscious mind is the private vault of one's consciousness. In it are stored all memory, the reserves of psychic power, what is commonly called "deep-seated feeling," the automated controls of our life activity. In one day we turn thousands of keys to thousands of locks to make deposits and withdrawals from this bank of self. It is the mind lock. The conscious mind is the watchman entrusted with the keys. So it is a wise person who continually asks self, "What am I locking in and what am I locking out?"

A student of Truth who reveres the spiritual way of life soon learns not to play around with soul regression, hypnotism, and psychic experimentation. Activity in these fields belongs to those who do responsible research and are specially qualified, working from a spiritual point of control rather than dabbling. Even in our normal awareness activity, thoughts and feelings are turning keys to the mind lock as fast as one can think and feel. The best keys are spiritual creative ideas and the Truths Jesus taught. He told His disciples to use spiritual keys for unlocking (withdrawing) and locking (depositing) the powers and energies with which consciousness is always involved. He said, "I will give you the keys of the kingdom of heaven, and whatever you loose on earth shall be loosed in heaven." This supports the statement that the kingdom of heaven is within the dimension of mind where we can expand our awareness of spiritual reality. We build our consciousness by the character of both our inner and outer life, because each interacts with the other.

We get back in our life experiences the character of what we put in, because consciousness demonstrates. Good, bad, or indifferent, we all ultimately must be responsible for what we bind and loose in dealing with the mind lock, the subconscious mind. How we exercise choice, commonly called free will, determines what will be demonstrated and experienced in the pattern and quality of our life. Although the spiritual keys are given to us, we need to decide individually how we will use them to bind and loose the powers and energies that relate to subconscious activity. This is the ancient wisdom found in the Biblical proverb: "Keep your heart with all vigilance; for from it flow the springs of life."

Conscious control requires deliberation before speaking and continual self-monitoring of what we are thinking. When a thought forms a judgment or decision, it becomes bound to the inner consciousness or programmed in the subconscious vault for later release. In our speech, emotions, and behavior, the character of that judgment and decision is loosed in the world of our personal life and affairs. The conscious mind provides a control center for what we are free to express this moment and for what may be expressed unconsciously later—to our own surprise—causing the familiar comment, "I didn't realize what I was saying at the time." It is important to keep in mind that the conscious mind acts in the present tense and the subconscious mind reacts from the past tense. This is perfect justice because we judge ourself and are free to change the character of our consciousness. Jesus was referring to this activity of mind when He said, "I tell you, on the day of judgment men will render account for every careless word they utter; for by your words you will be justified, and by your words you will be condemned."

Preoccupation of an intense, personal nature will lock too much concentrated psychic energy in the subconscious mind. Such repressed feeling "wants out," and the lock will then open involuntariy to give vent to inner feelings and frustration. The instinctive reactive nature of the subconscious mind to loose on earth what is bound within is testified to by the use of a polygraph, better known as a lie detector. A guilty person may have enough conscious control to answer verbally in terms of innocence by lying to a question, but the locked-in feeling and knowledge of one's guilt are released by the question and are manifested in a quickened heartbeat, high blood pressure, and excited respiratory action.

Taking this explanation one step further, it is easy to see how all repressed feelings of a negative nature or self-deprecation take their toll physically. Health, harmony, and peace in mind and body depend upon an input of good thoughts, positive concepts, self-confidence, and loving awareness all day long. In the evening, before falling asleep, lock good treasures in heaven's vault. Invest the best conscious thoughts you can in the subconscious bank.

Not only are we locking and unlocking, binding and loosing, the negative and positive, error and Truth, into the subjectivity of our personal consciousness; but we can through personal influence, suggestion, and thought transference have some effect upon others. A good example of this is what friends or family may feel when visiting someone at the hospital. To say, "You look so pale," "I imagine you dread these next few days," or, "I feel so sorry for you!" does not bless or uplift someone in a time of trial and anxiety. Many parents do not realize the importance of sending a child to bed in a happy state of mind. In the morning, a child going to school or a husband leaving for work will enjoy a better day if the exchange in this daily parting is one that turns the keys of love, appreciation, caring, and trusting. The keys literally dangle on the tongue and turn at the impulse of the heart's affection.

Jesus commented on this: "The spirit indeed is willing, but the flesh is weak." Quite simply, if the conscious desire is not strong or inclined to follow Spirit's ready guidance, the power to speak the Word is wasted at the human level. But we have the power to command. We have the right to choose what will be bound and loosed in heaven and on earth. The right use of psychic energies is found in how one exercises conscious control, thought by thought, not in tampering with the locks of the subconscious by playing games with the occult. God's good is infinite and God's grace is endless, but we still need to deal with the holdings of the subconscious mind. The accounts held in the mind lock need to be kept in order and through affirmation, right action, right thinking, prayer, and meditation can be balanced as we work at the level of conscious control.

The inviolability of your soul is in your own hands. You sit in the driver's seat. You work the combination and turn the keys. You have the keys of the kingdom of heaven and the freedom to bind and loose what you consciously choose to do and to be. "The good man out of the good treasure of his heart produces good, and the evil man out of his evil treasure produces evil; for out of the abundance of the heart his mouth speaks."

FROM KARMA TO GRACE

The traveler on the spiritual path quickly learns that man is under law and all things demonstrate through the process of "cause and effect." This premise is true as far as it applies, and gives foundation to the action of justice in our lives and affairs. There is a "wheel of justice" that encompasses us all in the turning events and circumstances of our lives. Yet something sublime from the heart of God permits man to transcend the law in times of great need and moments precious and rare. Faith with love ushers in the grace of God, and an extra dimension can be found beyond the law.

Eastern religions have promoted an elaborate and mature teaching about the law centuries before Christianity was born. The concept, still popular today, came from an ancient Sanskrit word we know as "karma." Karma literally means "destiny in action," the belief that each man is reincarnated to reap the rewards or the corrective consequences of his former life expression on earth. Unfortunately, preoccupation with this concept can very easily produce a sense of fatalism or incite too much fantasy in one's contemplation of lives past and lives to be.

A higher realization of God can lead to the experience of grace, that unexplainable happening which can instantly forgive and erase a debt burdening the soul. Paul pointed out to the Galatians: "Now before faith came, we were

40

confined under the law, kept under restraint until faith
should be revealed. So that the law was our custodian until
Christ came, that we might be justified by faith. But now
that faith has come, we are no longer under a custodian."
He made clear that, in our concern with working under
the law, we should appreciate how the transcendental
power of Christ within can be found to move from karma
to grace.

This distinction between the law and grace was dramat-
ically demonstrated in an outer way when Major Edward
White took a twenty-one minute "space walk" during the
four-day flight of Gemini IV, back in 1965. He was the
first American to float in free orbit, and something happened to him that nearly precipitated an out-of-this-
world crisis for anxious earthbound officials. It seems he
showed a reluctance to leave the intoxicating state of freedom he was enjoying. Only gentle but strong persuasion
brought him back to the ship. He returned with the comment, "It's the saddest moment of my life." Grace is the
love of the Creator toward us all, every living thing from
mineral to man as all life eternally evolves and is lifted
higher and higher. We can go around in circles under karma,
but grace lifts up the circle to make it a meaningful spiral-
ing action. The progessive spiral of life has each cycle transcending the former one. In this respect, the grace of God
is blessing and touching all our lives whether we recognize
the lifting-up activity or not. The revelation of help from
Jesus Christ for his conversion was interpreted by Paul
as the assurance to him, "My grace is sufficient for you."

Grace is exposure to a higher consciousness, just as
"free orbit" is found in the higher altitude. Whether we
leave the gravity of earth or the gravity of heavy, oppres-
sive thought, a weightlessness can immediately be sensed.
In fact, we feel singularly favored at such a time. Major
White no doubt felt he was blessed among all mankind
during those twenty-one minutes he was free of every
petty human involvement, unburdened by responsibilities
of a highly technical and demanding nature, unaware that
he had even an ounce of body weight.

The word *grace* is derived from the Latin *gratia*, meaning favor. In a time of exalted consciousness one has a right to feel divinely favored. Jesus apparently felt this when He heard the assurance, "This is my beloved Son, with whom I am well pleased." At the time He was baptized in the public recognition that He was a new prophet and teacher without equal. Such an experience brings an electric manifestation from Spirit. Call it divine inspiration, heavenly approval, revelation from God, or simply a "spiritual infilling." It is grace, and it transcends the law. Paul himself, when he lost his Pharisaic complex, never quite got over that wonderful memory of having received grace. It lingered on with him and years later, while during house arrest in Rome, he wrote the Philippians, "You are all partakers with me of grace."

Man is still struggling under law, not yet fully aware that the grace of God is constantly favoring him and lifting him up. But for the grace of God, which is always favoring us as His own, how would we know that there is so much more to self-identity, existence, and the creation that engulfs us?

A minister told a story about a member of his congregation who had traveled to a tropical area thousands of miles away. Some weeks later the minister received a letter from the man with just these five words, "A sample of my environment." That was all. Enclosed with the letter was a lovely, colorful, indescribably beautiful feather from a tropical bird. The communication was complete and never forgotten by the minister. No lenghty letter, eloquently worded, could have told so much about the correspondent's environment as an earthly place of paradise. Likewise, when we experience a moment of God's grace, that is what the Father is forever broadcasting through the dimness of our human consciousness: "a sample of My environment."

We need not feel bound to an endless cycle of karma, birth and rebirth, the crawling pace of cause and effect. Mistakenly, good-intentioned people may assiduously

discipline themselves until they become numb and un-
responsive to the gracious way of Spirit. Haven't you seen
someone so busy working with the law, struggling with
everything as though only his own effort counted, that
you could not speak a blessing to him and be heard—or
favor him with a smile and a gesture of heart-given warmth?

When I was a boy, there was a plaything, cylindrical
in shape and made of a basket weave, just large enough to
insert an index finger at either end. The ends were scalloped
like pointed teeth. If I inserted my fingers and pulled with
the least pressure to obtain release, this innocent-looking
gadget tightened uncomfortably and held me captive to
my own efforts. Only a gentle movement and subtle with-
drawal of one finger at a time brought release. It was a
"let go and let God" contrivance! The principle of its
action is a classic example of how to get the benefits of
grace, the higher action of God beyond the law.

Karma is only the conditioning of man until he finds
that higher activity in himself. Beyond the law there is
only love. Grace and love are synonymous terms and Paul's
personal testimony holds true for us all: "Love is the ful-
filling of the law." Love is the grace of God in action, personified by Jesus Christ's commandment: "Love one
another, even as I have loved you."

THE TENDRILS OF LIFE

My wife recently called me out of the house to join her on the patio. She had discovered something she calls "a lesson in Truth." Pointing to the needle-wide crack between two fence boards separating our ground from our neighbor's flower bed, she made me aware of a whole flowering plant, seemingly growing out of the fence two feet above the earth below. It was one of those things that go unnoticed and unquestioned until one realizes the paradox of the appearance. Closer examination revealed that a single stem, supporting the full growth on our side, was growing out of the larger body of a flowering shrub in our neighbor's yard. Some weeks back a small tendril worked its way through the slender crack, thickened, became wiry and strong, and produced the foliage we saw for one flower and buds about to bloom. And there it was, thriving as if suspended in air and rooted in the fence itself.

All growth seems to depend upon the tendrils of life. And the tendrils thicken and lengthen as they support more and more life. In birth our own life depends upon a slender connection, at first a tendril. We are attached to our mother by an umbilical cord, which is finally severed when we become physically independent from the cradle security of the womb. Even then an invisible connection seems to be evolving as a way for us to be nourished and sustained in the soul's earth-bound experience.

This is alluded to in the Book of Ecclesiastes, which contains twelve chapters of provocative wisdom. In the last chapter the writer, referrred to as the Preacher, speaks of the time "before the silver cord is snapped, . . . and the dust returns to the earth as it was, and the spirit returns to God who gave it." Many metaphysicians interpret the silver cord as meaning the vital connection holding the soul to the body, which when severed signifies the body's passing on beyond mortal ties. Did it begin and evolve as a tendril connection, continuing the life-giving function of the umbilical cord? The significance is more than symbolic. And beyond, there must be a tendril to which the soul is attached that will nourish, sustain, and perpetuate the transcending self on the immortal path.

Jesus taught a deep mystical truth regarding the universal Spirit, Christ, I AM, as the Source to which all spiritual identity is connected, branching out like a mother plant to bear tendrils of life inseparable from the Idea imaged in the seed. He said, "I am the true vine, and my Father is the vinedresser. Every branch of mine that bears no fruit, he takes away, and every branch that does bear fruit he prunes, that it may bear more fruit." Whether you think in terms of reincarnation, or simply life after death, this verse gives the unmistakable assurance that our growth goes on and that nothing is lost. It is all in keeping the invisible connection unbroken in consciousness: "He who abides in me, and I in him, he it is that bears much fruit, for apart from me you can do nothing."

Every thought is the tendril through which the God-Mind can feed us with love, wisdom, strength, the fullness of the Christ Self. Charles Fillmore taught that thought is the connecting link between God and man. And when we may feel separated in consciousness, a frail tendril thought which renews the contact can soon become a great channel through which Spirit can flow. Man needs his divine attachment, for without it he is nothing.

Here in the Southwest where I live, there are times when the air-conditioner, dishwasher, refrigerator, electric range, television, and overhead lights all defy talk of an "energy shortage," simply because a single main wire connects our home with pure power and distributes the power wherever it is claimed. If the main line is broken, everything stops. Yet it can be restored, and all is then as though nothing ever happened. During an electrical storm, when a main line is down, we appreciate the importance of that single connection.

Emilie Cady teaches in *Lessons in Truth* that human suffering results from one's sense of separation from God. This can only be in the error of consciousness, when the individual abides too much in the outer self and loses contact with his inner Christ. One tendril of faith, of love, of understanding can always begin the growth process again and cause the consciousness to flourish and flower.

No matter how "fenced in" a person may feel, he can send forth a tendril thought that will bear fruit—the fruit of the Spirit filling the consciousness with the abundant life. There must be contact, a connection. Organic life finds a way through the tendrils of a root system and the tendrils of new shoots. Is the plant of man's consciousness any different? No power on earth can resist the tendril of love or faith reaching to express throughout the universe, knowing no boundaries. From the finite self we bridge mortal limitations when we take the life of the vine into the tendril. We are the branches of "the true vine" called I AM. And our garden grows thought by thought, tendril by tendril. We live by the tendrils of life.

WHEN I AM STILL

There is a time of solitude
    Called prayer, a place apart,
When I find inner quietude
    And Christ within my heart.

There is a place where I may go
    Away from doubt and strife,
Where He my every need does know—
    The Comforter of life.

The Christ of God now stirs in me
    As momently I pray,
And I find closer unity
    With Him each passing day.

My prayers, my thoughts, now seem as one
    Expression of His will,
So lovingly His work is done
    Whenever I am still.

LOVE'S COUNTENANCE

Love is present everywhere,
    A gentle face without a care
That looks more innocent and mild
    Than shyness in a little child.

Love is Christ within us now,
    His presence showing mankind how
Twelve men were taught humility—
    Whose feet He washed at Bethany.

Love is a power in the heart
    To bind all men who are apart.
We first must love to find release,
    A consciousness of heaven's peace!

Love serves all humanity—
    The call of Christ is "Follow me"—
And we His countenance can bear,
    A gentle face without a care.

UNTIL WE BLOOM

All the filaments of the root
Are vital to the upward shoot,
And spread their network underground
Until the root is tightly bound.

Creation wisely uses earth
To give identity its birth;
The genesis of life's ascent
Brings forth the bud and fragrant scent.

In this spiral of transcending,
Human form is not an ending—
The world is but a cosmic womb
And nurtures us until we bloom.

MEDITATION

I acknowledge the Spirit of Truth, forever active in the realm of inner consciousness. Now I give my awareness to experience the pure revelation of divine insight. "The true light that enlightens every man . . . shines in the darkness" and I inwardly sense the infiltration of Its illumining power. There is a dawning in my soul and I behold the spiritual sunrise. I am aware of higher planes of reality. I realize there are "many mansions" where I may abide as a divine guest.

The indwelling Divine "I" glorifies my shadow self. Great truths from all scriptures ever written, from all inspired poets, teachers, writers and saints merge as One Truth and sanctify my memory. It is as though Jesus spoke to me when he said: "When the Spirit of truth comes, he will guide you into all the truth."

The divine message of every tongue proves to be timeless and subject to translation by the ear of the heart. Every thread of wisdom, love and inspiration weaves a noble design in the tapestry of sacred thought. The Word that illumined Buddha, embodied divine wisdom in the Upanishads, was made flesh in Jesus, which feeds those who hunger and thirst for righteousness, declares a creed common to all and is Self-revealing. I am assured, "To you it has been given to know the secrets of the kingdom of God."

At rest in the Silence, I know "I AM" is God— forever teaching me through my Divine "I" within. I am grateful to know I will reach sublime heights. In this dawn of my becomingness, I sense the whole day of eternity before me. I walk in the Light. I learn. I aspire to be perfect and every step on the path glorifies my soul.

50

II
INSIGHTS OF HEALTH, HEALING
AND WELL-BEING

SUCH AS I HAVE

Where does a miracle begin? How is it empowered? This is dramatized in a very moving, convincing account in the Bible. The conviction most needed today is that "miracles never cease." Time cannot and has not changed the power of God. I have personally read in the daily newspapers reports of the blind having their sight restored after many years; the rare instances of a terminal health condition regressing; the handicapped able to walk again; even astounding stories by those who claim to have come back to life on this plane after what was pronounced death.

In every normal healing there is the truth that life is always restoring, renewing, regenerating, seeking to bring forth the wholeness of the Creator in each creation, whether the form of life is a microbe or a human being. The miraculous recoveries, healings, and demonstrations testify to more than a spontaneity of action. There is the will to believe, faith, acceptance, receptivity and heightened expectancy.

In Acts we find the portrayal of the healing of a lame man who stood at the gate to the temple. Before going into an interpretation of this account, let us read from Acts 3:1-8:

"Now Peter and John were going up to the temple at the hour of prayer, the ninth hour. And a man lame from birth was being carried, whom they laid daily at the gate of the temple which is called Beautiful to ask alms of those who entered the temple. Seeing Peter and John about to go into the temple, he asked for alms. And Peter directed his gaze at him, with John, and said, 'Look at us.' And he fixed his attention upon them, expecting to receive something from them. But Peter said, 'I have no silver and gold, but I give you what I have; in the name of Jesus Christ of Nazareth, walk.' And he took him by the right hand and raised him up; and immediately his feet and ankles were made strong. And leaping up he stood and walked and entered the temple with them, walking and leaping and praising God."

The miracle began with Peter's faith that the man might be able to walk with sufficient encouragement. The miracle was empowered by Peter's emphatic desire to help, to literally uplift the lame man. He gave the most precious gift of all, "what I have." What a turnabout for someone wanting only a handout rather than compassion, spiritual aid, or comfort! Peter had quickly made it clear that he and John were not a soft touch, had nothing of material value to offer. It was not a casual brushoff, because Peter fastened his eyes upon the lame man, an eye contact that no doubt reached into the beggar's very soul. The man sensed the unmistakable climax of the moment, the implied invitation that suggested the supernatural. "He fixed his attention upon them, expecting to receive something from them." The eloquence and literary excellence of what Peter then said is a verse one can scarcely forget, here quoted from the King James Version: " 'Silver and gold have I none; but such as I have give I thee: In the name of Jesus Christ of Nazareth rise up and walk.' " He even took the man by his right hand in the gesture of raising him up. The result was miraculous! He surely made an inner contact, an empathic bond that stirred the lame man to use of himself the "such as I have." It sounds so ambiguous to say," such as I have," yet to give, to use, to appreciate the least essence we can identify with consciously within ourself sets in action the innate powers of Spirit; it empowers a miracle to happen.

It is so tragic in our world today that intense personal preoccupation with material needs, dependency upon the things of life rather than on the power of Spirit fixes our attention to the limitation of appearances. We are all somewhat crippled in consciousness by measuring what is possible by our human scales—weighing on the fulcrum of limited reason and unimaginative logic. In our own way, we can be standing outside the gate of the temple of life, feeling unable to enter into the fullness of the whole Spirit. We want God to give us something and we send out beseeching prayers, although all the while the "such as I have" waits to be recognized and accepted. Sometimes we need the encouragement of a loved one, friend, or even a stranger to be mindful of the inner gift, and awakened from a deadened or lethargic state of consciousness toward the vital realization of life and its greater action empowered by our own faith.

Jesus employed direct spiritual psychology, repeatedly telling those who sought healing to rise up, to do something, "take up your bed and go home."

All Truth teachers know that the first acquaintance new students have with a powerful affirmation is that the positive statement works miraculously in the area of life where it is most needed. Later, as one settles into a less expectant state of mind, the rightness of new ideas is lost to human complacency, and the gift of "such as I have" seems to lose its Christmas magic, its breathtaking air of spring, its true innate value. We all need the instruction Paul gave to Timothy," rekindle the gift of God that is within you."

Thinking of yourself, the answer to the question of where a miracle begins, is quite simply with "such as I have." Peter initiated the action that brought a spontaneous response from the lame man. Something must happen in the subjectivity of the soul, it cannot be forced upon another person. Revival meetings can excite a response. A quiet prayer time alone can work a miracle. It can happen in the will and desire of an innocent child's mind.

In my early boyhood my older brother was paralyzed by polio. For weeks he could not walk. The family doctor, who in those days made his house calls with a frequency unbelievable today, came and went. As the waiting period lengthened, a grim resignation to face the worst while hoping for the best, was apparent. One morning I saw my brother take a few steps. I rushed downstairs and with bright, excited eyes proclaimed, "Harry is walking!" One might say that God's will prevailed, nature's healing work triumphed, or Harry was one of the "lucky" ones. No one really knows how much Harry took the affirmative, in his child's sense of challenge with the flesh, and resolved in his spirit to go all the way with "such as I have."

Each time I watch the track and field events of the Olympics I marvel at how an extra effort calls forth just that little bit more of the "such as I have" to break a world record or finish in first place. The factor of faith in oneself far overshadows the spirit of competition.

The poet Robert Browning gave an insight into how far one can go with only a fraction of the whole thing. He wrote, "On the earth the broken arcs; in heaven, the perfect round." Follow an arc on the exact curve of its bend and it will end its destination in a perfect circle. Work with any inspiration and the spark of an idea is ignited into full realization.

Jesus always praised the principle of faith that works with the "such as I have." He spoke of working with even the least measure of your faith, "as a grain of mustard seed." He saw greater virtue in the widow who gave her small offering, the "widow's mite" of two copper coins, as more in spiritual value than those who easily gave larger sums. "Truly, I say to you, this poor widow has put in more than all those who are contributing to the treasury. For they all contributed out of their abundance; but she out of her poverty has put in everything she had, her whole living." The demonstration of everything we seek to

accomplish begins with our using such as we have in the
conscious measure of our faith, love, strength, or whatever
the quality of spirit.

The father of a friend of mine came to New York City
early this century. He was a Russian Jew, escaping one of
the pogroms then underway. He arrived in America penni-
less, the typical immigrant of his time, alone in a strange
and awesome land. Somehow he got started in our free
enterprise system selling pencils and stationery on the side-
walks of New York. From small sales, he built up his
meager inventory. Gradually he took on new lines, up-
graded his business, and went into new fields of selling.
Years passed and he prospered. He went into food processing. During World War II the government made large pur-
chases of his products. Toward retirement he lived on
Park Avenue and his educated son handled much of his
correspondence, because he still spoke what is termed
"broken English." He had invested the mite of his inven-
tories again and again. He had followed the arc that led to
the perfect round of success. He had nourished the seeds
of faith in himself. He had worked the miracle of "such as
I have."

How does a miracle begin? How is it empowered? Life
is filled with miracles that never cease. They begin in the
first impulse of faith, are empowered by what we accept
and expect beyond what appears. The secret ingredient of
every miracle is the "such as I have." We can work up
miracles for ourself, and we can give of that inner ingredient to help others. Emerson said, "Unless I stand on
higher ground, how can I lift up my brother? Peter and
John stood on that higher ground at the gate of the temple
which is called "Beautiful" when the lame man was healed
by the spoken word of Truth, the giving of the greatest
gift one can give to another.

Life's temple invites us to enter in. Its gate is the portal
between existing and living, and it is beautiful. The hand
of faith reaches out, sometimes in our own inner believing
and sometimes from another soul, but always it is the hand

of God. When love accompanies faith (because Peter personified faith and John was the disciple of love), all the spiritual powers for demonstration are there to use the "such as I have." Miracles begin right were we are. Miracles will never cease. We should work with what we have in our own spirituality, to enjoy our share, and walk through that gate called "Beautiful" into the temple of life.

RELAX AND LIVE

The ability to relax opens the mind and heart to all God has to offer us. Because the kingdom of God is truly within us, our thoughts and feelings must be relaxed and receptive to the inner peace, joy, health, security, and the heavenly order, if we are to realize them in our lives. This is the way to "inherit the kingdom prepared for [us] from the foundation of the world."

When one feels life is a burden and the load is too heavy, the result is tension, and brings the feeling of inadequacy, of being unequal to the responsibility of it all. So many of us literally fall into this type of thinking simply because we still struggle to overcome human tendencies.

No one really knows what he is capable of until he completely relaxes. We underestimate our inner strength and resourcefulness for applying spiritual methods to worldly problems. Time and again I have observed in myself and in others how far we exceed ourselves whenever we express a relaxed state of mind in meeting the personal demands made upon us.

Someone has said that "the mind is like a bow, the stronger by being unbent." A good archer never really stretches his bow beyond the test of its strength. He knows exactly when he has pulled to the point of maximum stretch for the control and accuracy desired. As quickly as he reaches that point, he returns to a relaxed position. So it is in our thinking. No one can be a bent bow all the time! If he is, people will surely comment, "If only he would unbend a little."

In today's fast moving society, too many of us occasionally fit the description of the Red Queen in *Alice's Adventures in Wonderland*. She was quoted as making this nervous declaration, "I have to keep running all the time just to stand still." Nothing betrays an unrelaxed mind so much as one's conversation.

We all need to practice relaxed conversation to receive the right responses from others. The flower of pure communication will not unfold unless it is released from strain and anxiety. Just think of a tight rosebud. Could it ever bloom without going through a phase of relaxation in the growth process, each petal unfolding gently by itself?

Relaxation is as essential to our well-being and spiritual growth as breathing, eating, and sleeping are to our physical health. When we relax we get our best ideas and deeper insights for happy, successful living. The subconscious mind works more efficiently through a relaxed conscious mind. Whenever we get still, let go of tense personal thoughts, there is a beneficial response from our inner self.

When Jesus invited his followers to come apart awhile, to unburden themselves and take on a more spiritual awareness of life, he assured them, "ye shall find rest unto your souls." This means relaxation is not complete until the soul itself is relaxed, and an inner freedom from strain, pressure, and tension is achieved.

All the organs of the body, like the heart and lungs, are of relaxable, plastic substance and form. Could we breathe with lungs fashioned of ivory? How long would the valves of the heart last if they were brittle tubes of bone? That is why relaxation is healing and permits us to receive the life-stream of energy and its ultimate and perfect expression. Relaxation allows no obstruction. As Charles Fillmore once said, "We find that relaxation of the tense abdomen depends on relaxation of the tense will."

When the heart tenses it will not let the blood pump through because the pulmonary artery becomes constricted. So receive all that is life-giving—blood, energy, ideas, the inner bread of life—we must relax. Letting go and letting God is the way to inherit the kingdom of God that is within us.

Let's practice relaxation, then health, happiness, and harmony flow from the spiritual movement of life within us. As we let go of thought burdens, unload tensions and pressures, we might well affirm these words of the Psalmist: "Create in me a clean heart, O God; and renew a right spirit within me."

TAKE A HEALING WALK

Has anyone ever told you to "Go take a walk" as a playful brush-off or because you have have persisted on an unwelcome subject?

If so, have you considered how beneficial such advice can be if followed literally?

In counseling there are times when I prescribe taking a walk as an immediate spiritual treatment. This prescription is not a substitute for prayer. I merely recommend this experience as an aid to positive and prayerful activity.

Many persons who have received this counsel were "holed up" in a room or apartment, or in a confining mental state of mind where a fretful and worrisome attitude was inhibiting the natural, relaxed, creative expression of prayer.

Walking can be an exercise of one's whole being, an exercise we can usually engage in to some degree regardless of the problem we may be working out. Walking demonstrates freedom of movement, stimulates circulation, widens the horizon, and cleanses away mental negation.

In taking a walk to think things over and become receptive to God's guidance, countless marriages have been saved and infinite tides of negation turned.

I never fail to receive inspiration from observing the wonderful ways people go about living a practical life of

Truth. There was a retired school teacher who came quite regularly to one of my morning classes. She had no car and never took a bus that I could observe.

As I became better acquainted with her, I once offered her a ride to her end of town on a day that I happened to be going that way. With a polite refusal, she explained that she loved to walk. I have never forgotten her proud statement: "I walked my way to health out of sickness."

This statement carried a lot of authority, for she had then walked a life span of 75 years on this earth, and just to attend this class she traveled on foot 18 city blocks back and forth, week after week, under hot summer suns and through winter snows. Naturally, she was actively walking all during the week, and walking with the freedom to be expected of a much younger person.

This dear lady is but one of countless men and women who have developed this pattern of living. I love to hear their testimonials of how walking has become a spiritual exercise and a spiritual experience. In consciously walking with an awareness of God's presence, it takes on healing power.

Jesus Walked Much

The record of Jesus' health is very clear. He obviously transmitted an aura of health and strength as He sought to bless others. In the three years of His ministry recorded in the Gospels, I am certain He walked more miles than most men His age walk these days from the day they are born. He walked mountain paths and rough-surfaced, dusty roads, and in a hot climate. And air-cushioned soles were nonexistent then.

Consider the depth of Jesus' meditative powers, the invigorating flow of renewing life forces, the sense of oneness with God quickened as He walked long hours from town to town, long days from city to city, long weeks and months from province to province. Surely, the walking and praying became fused until they became as one activity of the soul; and therein I think we can find a simple clue to what is often mysteriously called His mystical life.

Paul, as he roamed about the Roman Empire, had no private car, not even a bicycle.

A photograph of a Cleveland minister in gym clothes appeared in a newspaper. He was in the middle of a stride around an indoor YMCA track. He had celebrated his 60th birthday with the announcement that he had run 2,700 miles, working out three times a week by running a five-mile stretch each time. He declared that he considered the body the temple of the soul, and he took physical fitness seriously.

Do you?

Do you walk enough to fulfill your prayers for health and strength and freedom from confinement?

The important thing is not whether your walk is only one block or a five-mile run; the important thing is to demonstrate the ability you have to be an active, vital person. If it is in your power to walk even to some degree, then develop this activity that can help regenerate the body and renew the mind, and can cause you to notice the stars.

No Better Medicine

Early morning dawn and early evening dusk are enchanted hours, if you will share them with the universe.

Aware of the words, "Physician, heal yourself," I take an evening walk with my wife. We walk two or three miles together. There is no better medicine for strain, sluggishness, or mental preoccupation. Hours of physical inactivity or daily routine can be balanced by walking with the freedom of Spirit.

"Enoch walked with God," and that is our privilege too! The secret is to walk in the light, the light of God. Think of your steps as synchronizing with mental steps on an inner stairway leading up to spiritual heights of consciousness. Walk with a light heart and for the sheer joy of it.

I always admired Mohandas Gandhi because he walked hundreds of miles, even as Jesus walked, in his love for life and mankind. This little bespectacled man in loincloth, with a taste for simple material things, secure in having "treasure in heaven," was blessed with perfect health and a pair of firm, well-molded legs. He was still young though in his 70's and had he not been assassinated no doubt would still be walking, pacifying, teaching, loving, and exerting a healing influence in India and upon the world.

The principle of life is harmonious activity. One begins with what one can do now. If you are lying in a hospital bed unable to walk physically, envision yourself walking. Plan your first step. Anticipate it. Rise up within yourself to the freedom you always have within so that that freedom can be translated through cells, nerves, muscles, and limbs to demonstrate the command, "Rise and walk."

Jesus taught us to "Walk while you have the light." Paul said we could "Walk by the Spirit." Throughout the Bible walking is referred to as a symbol of spiritual mobility and mastery. You walk in Spirit when your thoughts keep in step with Truth, never letting human incidents throw you off stride.

Walk in the Light

There seems to be a ratio between health and walking. Many primitive people express health and an ability to survive despite poor diets, lack of proper sanitation, and unthinkable social handicaps because they are on their feet walking and working far more than modern man, who drives everywhere, sinks into his easy chair every night, and forgets one of the basic activities he is constituted to enjoy —walking.

So I prescribe that you take a healing walk.

Consciously resist the desire to slump away your life. Get out and see beyond four walls.

Greet the sun in the morning and the moon at night.

The way to health may lead out the door of your room or apartment, and out of too much preoccupation with your personal self.

Even if you are regarded as a shut-in, begin to walk in the light, in the garden of spiritual consciousness. God will be with you if you can get your thoughts in step with the idea that knowing Truth makes you free.

An imaginary walk, strengthened by faith on the feet of understanding, calls forth a physical response in the regeneration of the body. I frequently hear firsthand testimony from faithful students of Truth who have walked their way to health. They got started by walking first in the light of the mind as they glimpsed the radiant life of Christ within.

I believe the soul soars when the body walks under the influence of one's faith and awareness of God as the guiding presence. Somehow, walking often leads to a spiritual experience, even though such an experience was not sought at the outset.

Why not treat yourself? Take a walk—a healing walk!

THE TRUE YOGA

A branch from the tree of Hinduism has been transplanted in North America and has taken root. It is known as Yoga. Yogic principles and exercises are being popularized as a kind of reverse missionary trend. Adherents come from all backgrounds in searching for a new physical culture, mysticism, weight control, and Truth. On first acquaintance with this practice and teaching, new and novel to most Western minds, it would seem unique and original to our Christian way of thinking. I would suggest that, to the contrary, there is a true yoga found in all great religions and especially in ours. Just as there is a diamond mine in Arkansas as well as those in South Africa, there is the same precious gem of truth in Christianity that is found in Hinduism. The true yoga is the crystal concept of one's relationship to the Spirit of God within.

Yoga is defined in the dictionary as meaning "union." It is derived from a Sanskrit word, and traced from old English origin we find it disguised in the familiar word *yoke*. This may immediately recall the words of Jesus as found in the eleventh chapter of Matthew: "Take my yoke upon you, and learn from me; for I am gentle and lowly in heart, and you will find rest for your souls. For my yoke is easy, and my burden is light." Now read these verses again and by substituting the word *union* for *yoke*,

66

a simple interpretation gives deeper meaning and dimension to Jesus' words. He was speaking of the mystical union one can find in oneness with Christ, linked self to Spirit as disciple to master Teacher.

I read not long ago that in Philadelphia alone there were ninety yoga classes. A yoga class is featured in a small store-front building just a few blocks from my home. In large cities most of the central YWCAs and YMCAs and their branches include yoga classes in their programs dedicated to health and universal brotherhood. Numerous paperbacks can be identified everywhere by titles that capitalize "YOGA" in bold print. How many secret inquirers or followers there are can only be estimated as considerable.

There is the most practiced form of yoga, known as Hatha Yoga, the physical method of assuming various beneficial postures known as "asanas." There can be no doubt that properly practiced this can lead to more body tone, harmony of mind and body, and a type of relaxation promoting meditation experiences. A person who plays with children at their games and will assume floor postures, natural and childlike, knows yoga unconsciously. Fishing, walking, doing many things in a relaxed yet controlled involvement with body, mind, and spiritual awareness results in yoga for those who know the experience. So there is the yoga of the East and the yoga of the West. The true yoga is simply union with God in the posture of body, mind, and soul. In spirit the East and the West do meet (with due respect to Rudyard Kipling).

Yogic principles that teach deeper spiritual truths have their parallel in the Bible. The yogi strongly believes in "prana," the vital breath of spirit of life-giving substance. The Bible has many references to "breath of life" and "breath of God." The Christian concept of the Holy Spirit implies this as practically doctrinal in all denominations. One of the most moving performances of blessing others is found in the Gospel of John, where it is said of Jesus speaking to His disciples, "He breathed on them, and said to them, Receive the Holy Spirit."

Not too long ago a news item reported that surgeons in New Haven, Connecticut, had implanted an electronic pacer in the neck of a Canadian teen-ager to solve a rare and unusual problem: he had to think consciously about breathing or his breathing would stop. When I read this, I thought of how yoga stresses conscious breathing and physical-mental control leading toward spiritual union. The emphasis on ecology makes this an even more timely consideration. We should not take "the breath of life" for granted, and yoga is to be commended for reminding Christians of this concept of old, testified to by our prophets and great teachers. In Truth there is one yoga, but there are many approaches and forms and practices.

An old Russian proverb states, "Wherever there is a neck there is a yoke." So we should take the yoke offered us by our higher Christ Self, to learn meekness and find rest for our soul. One cannot live without a conscious tie with God, spiritual union, a sense of that "higher love." We should practice the postures of mind that Jesus Christ taught, as in the Beatitudes. As we consciously partake of the spiritual substance, the omnipresent spiritual body, regeneration is experienced. Jesus repeated to His disciples a tenet of Judaism, "Man does not live by bread alone." On another occasion He referred to the subtle spiritual essence of life He could appropriate by affirming, "I have food to eat of which you do not."

Yogic principles help us to see basic truths in our own culture, though they are not kept secret. By a tolerant and understanding comparison of religions, it is easy to see beyond apparent differences. In fact, there is an old Vedic hymn of the Hindus, held sacred centuries before Christianity was born, which translated reads: "As different streams having their sources in different places mingle their waters in the sea, so, O Lord, the different paths men take through different tendencies, various though they appear, crooked or straight, all lead to Thee."

The old story about finding acres of diamonds in one's own backyard, figuratively speaking, applies in searching for the true yoga. Geography, culture, history—nothing of this world can keep one from the revelation of how to find true spiritual union. There is a consummate bliss one can instinctively find by seeking right where he was born, and in using the best of his background he will find that "a rose is a rose is a rose is a rose." We can be thankful when the missionaries from the East show us another arrangement of the rose's beauty and caption it with their own way of appreciation. It is to be hoped that America's hungering and thirsting for spiritual experiences will regenerate a deeper insight into the Scriptures. "Whoever drinks of the water that I shall give him will never thirst; but the water that I shall give will become in him a spring of water welling up to eternal life."

THE ALCHEMY OF THOUGHT

When one first walks on the spiritual path there comes an inner conviction, intuitively revealed, that thought has transforming power. Whether you call yourself metaphysician, Truth student, or simply Christian, thought is the tool of mind. Each person has the built-in ability to think; and, as is the case with any tool, thought is essential to fulfill the purpose of its use. The right use of thought as a tool will open the mind, unlocking new doors of awareness for higher self-expression.

Have you ever equated the universal Mind of God (and your individual mind) with someone working in the laboratory of creation? Every soul is working, researching, making its own discoveries in the great workshop called life. We might compare ourself to the alchemists of medieval times. Although they were often portrayed in ridiculous ways, they were not really wizards wearing high, conical headgear decorated with stars. Early alchemists had a wonderful dream of transforming base metals into gold. In pursuit of that dream they worked tirelessly in search and experimentation, producing many discoveries beneficial to all mankind. The science of chemistry was born with them, and they enjoyed continued success in other areas of science, even though their original goal was not realized.

Alchemists made many practical discoveries. From their research came the knowledge of dyes, metallurgy, optical lenses, and much more. Their counterparts, the astrologers, dreamed of revealing the future through prophetic reading of the celestial bodies. Like the alchemists, they never quite achieved their ideal, but they stimulated the science of astronomy. Although astrology still captures the imagination, it is wise to remember the saying, "The stars may impel us, but they cannot compel us."

Today's "alchemists" are research scientists and industrial engineers. They have produced synthetic rubber, diamonds, and gems, plastic substitutes of a thousandfold purposes. There is a clear similarity between all of us who work in the laboratory of our mind. We seek to transform the base elements of human nature, the primal instincts, the lingering states of primitive consciousness, into the golden ideal of perfect self. We persist with the alchemist in a tireless, dedicated quest for the ultimate dream made true.

Occasionally a single electrifying thought turns the key in an outburst of faith and brings great blessings. One name for such a result is *miracle*. This was recently demonstrated to me while I was visiting a woman who had been struggling with extreme arthritis and dependency upon a walker and cane. As she lay in bed one morning, about to get up, thinking of the ordeal of simply getting around from place to place, she suddenly focused on the healing miracle of the paralyzed man who was told by Jesus to take up his bed and walk. The woman told me that a great realization came over her, and she said to herself, "If He could do it then, I can do it now!" That moment she got up, walked without artificial aid, and continued to so for several months.. That is the alchemy of thought at work. It has transforming power. What great energy and potential can move through the right thought to spark great action!

One strong thought can begin a career, cause a move of thousands of miles, reconcile extreme differences, or inspire one to write an article. If we trust the transforming power of thought, we can turn the key with faith. Like the step that begins a journey, one right thought can start a wonderful demonstration of life fulfillment.

Carl Jung, the psychiatrist, spoke of the "energetics of the soul." What did he mean? If a single atom has an energy field, the soul with its body of trillions of atoms in a highly organized form has its own glorious field of energy. Thought is the lever that activates our atomic power. Studies into the existence of electromagnetic fields now indicate that everyone has an L-field (life field) and a T-field (thought field). These energy fields represent the indestructible body of our consciousness. Cells and molecules come and go, are constantly being replaced, but the energy fields for each person are stable and enduring. We express through these fields as we exercise directive thought and initiate action in our thinking-feeling nature. We are offered possibilities of expression beyond all imagination. Referring to our potential for development, Dr. Marcus Bach has said, "I am not asking you to do the impossible, I am asking you to do the possible untried."

Primitive man, the aborigine struggling for survival, instinctively knew that his thought activated a power. Perhaps he regarded this power as something outside himself and revered it by his superstitions, totems, taboos, and rituals. But more and more mankind sensed the energetics of the soul and directly expressed creatively with an awakening faith, working with God as the power within. In this workshop of life, in the laboratory of self, we find the Mind of God extending to the filament of our own thought. By working consciously with thought as a tool—the key that opens doors to new awareness and greater expression of the soul—we become co-workers with God in the great laboratory of creation itself.

More than two hundred references to righteousness in the Bible indicate that the true virtue of thought is its transforming power. Why? Because righteousness implies right use, and those many passages record how righteousness prevails. There is scientific proof that affirmations of health, faith, love, any desired state of being, can cause energized response. Every thought has the potential to activate deeper dimensions of self. We recognize this in ourself and in others as our life and thought fields touch and merge in affinity. Then how careful we must be when a rapport of sensitivity is expressed, because we are dealing with atomic power.

At the height of the Hellenistic culture in Alexandria, Egypt, intelligent people believed there was a substance which, if found, could transmute all baser metal into gold. This substance was known as the philosopher's stone. It gave great impetus to their searching, which hastened progress in arts, skills, and trades. Man accomplishes very little without an ideal, a goal that seems to be beyond him.

The metaphysician, the Truth student, the Christian have an ideal to seek within—the Christ. The Christ is not merely a man, a passing myth, but the true inner divine Identity. When our thought touches the Spirit of Christ within, we experience transforming power. So we should respect the energetics of the soul, the life field and the thought field. In giving our thought to healing, prosperous, loving, harmonizing, spiritual ideas, great things will be wrought using the power of faith. Jesus has challenged us to "do the possible untried" through the alchemy of thought. His words still echo the assurance, "All things are possible to him who believes."

EMPATHY

There is word called **empathy**—
The opposite of apathy.
It means you deeply feel and care
Enough your total self to share.

You can speak forth this inner gift
To give another soul a lift—
Like Peter, set a lame man free,
"Such as I have give I thee."

MIRACLE CALLED SPRING

Tendrils climb in exploration,
   Deep roots increase their hold;
Everywhere there's restoration
   As nature grows more bold.

The greening time transforms the earth,
   Tight buds burst into bloom—
We see the magic of new birth,
   Smell nature's sweet perfume.

God sends this miracle called spring
   To resurrect the soul.
Its magic moves the heart to sing,
   "I am alive and whole!"

MEDITATION

I surrender my soul to the Silence that pervades my inner being of self. There I hear that "still small voice" declare "Behold, I make all things new." In this transcendent awareness, my mind is purified, my heart is impassioned by a higher love, and the vitality of the Whole Spirit ministers to every mental, physical and environmental need. Restored, renewed and strengthened, I am content.

This quiet interlude penetrates the veil of outer appearances. I become reconciled with the momentary existence that builds the spiritual body change after change. Now I see that the eternal reality moves through the temporal patterns of yesterday, today, and tomorrow. I realize an inner perfection transforming outer imperfection closer to Its own ideal. My human resistance gives way to a spiritual acceptance—"now is the acceptable time."

Health is my divine nature. Healing is always taking place. My well-being is assured as I simply trust and cooperate with Spirit's perfect work. I feel the divine effluence. Life expands outward though me to renew the form. Love unifies all that has lost its sense of harmony. Light restores my mind to true understanding.

I see myself as a life-giving spirit. I am forever transformed by the renewing of my mind. The divine process proves the perfect will of God. I yield to spiritual quickening and my mind, body and affairs are made new. I will to be whole! With gratitude and ineffable joy in my heart, I give thanks for my health, healing and well-being.

III

INSIGHTS INTIMATE, PERSONAL AND UNIVERSAL

CONSCIOUSNESS COMMUNICATES

Words are symbols of thought, and their use through all media of expression was never more widespread than today. On television, over radio, by telephone, in print, the output of words to communicate was never greater. Modern man has all the outer ways and means, but too often the inner feeling seems to be lacking.

No message is ever truly helpful unless it delivers the realization one wishes to communicate. According to legend, if one had a heart-to-heart talk with someone in King Arthur's day, he said, "I discovered myself unto him." This was a simple testimony of having reached a mutual inner understanding.

The great Jewish philosopher and poet Martin Buber was famous for his principle of thinking in terms of "I-Thou" rather than "I-It," "I-She," or "I-He." He made a point of addressing a person and listening to a person as a spiritual individual, not as a teacher, housewife, foreigner, child, or illiterate, or as someone to be mentally fitted into a limited, narrow role or character. Prayer is often unsatisfactory because of the human inclination to picture God in some arbitrary, unrealistic relationship to oneself. Men and women seem to live by a social division, picturing each other as handicapped because of traits associated with their gender. Naturally, communication fails when consciousness reflects judgment, prejudice, or immaturity.

Life is an infinite communication system. The universe

is continually conversing within itself. Shakespeare described this when he wrote:

"Tongues in trees, books in the running brooks,
Sermons in stones, and good in everything."

This is literally true! Stones tell a geologist the age of civilization, the history of our planet's evolution, and many things that they radiate to his sensitive recorders. Radio astronomers learn more about outer space by listening with radio telescopes than was formerly learned by looking through observatory telescopes. Trees record each year by a growth ring that even indicates the kind of weather endured. There is communicability built into everything, mineral, vegetable, animal, and the soul of man.

In the realm of his consciousness, man can truly communicate with God. The Bible tells us "Be still and know that I am God." Brother Lawrence wrote, "There is not in the world a kind of life more sweet and delightful than that of a continual conversation with God." All communication is possible with the right conductor or attunement, be it a Geiger counter, radio telescope, or simply the very sensitive faculty of the heart each of us possesses.

Hardly a week passes but I experience proof of what many call mental telepathy. I am sure this happens to everyone. You expect a phone call and the person calls, or you call that person and are told you were especially in his thoughts that day. Thoughts do broadcast from heart to heart, through the subconscious intercom. They communicate even though we think we keep them in check.

Haven't you stopped before speaking a thought you felt was too trivial or irrelevant to put into words, only to find that someone got the message? My wife picks me up on this frequently. It is not a matter of reading my facial expression. We can be in bed with the lights out, ready to doze off; and when I inhibit a thought, she invariably asks, "What is it? You were about to say something."

The late Frank Buchman, founder of the Moral Re-Armament movement, had a wonderful way of explaining how God communication comes to man and broadcasts its directive throughout the universe when he prays for peace. He said: "When man listens, God speaks. When man obeys, God acts. When men change, nations change."

So the first step in creative communication begins in consciousness, seeking the spiritual instruction, the divine guidance from within. Job forgot this when he was struggling with his adversities. At the time, he listened to his own doubting thoughts and the opinions of well-meaning friends. Finally, his friend Elihu saw the dilemma and told Job, "There is a spirit in man, And the breath of the Almighty giveth them understanding."

Consciousness communicates, how much more richly from Divine Mind than from any other heart center. The conductor is an open mind and a receptive heart, knowing God in the "I-Thou" relationship rather than on narrow personal levels.

The second step in creative communication is to expect God to show you the great opportunity in your life that is tailor-made for your abilities and your circumstances. Right answers should fit one like a suit made to size. George Washington Carver learned this when he persisted in his scientific inquiry to ask God for the secrets of the universe. It was presumptuous of him; and finally his prayer was answered by the divine revelation which told him, "George, I can't give you the secrets of the universe, but I can give you the secrets of the peanut." Dr. Carver then communed with God at the heart of the peanut. He found a lifetime involvement in his discoveries and revolutionized the agriculture of the South, putting the secrets of the peanut to practical use for food and industry.

The third step in creative communication is to continue speaking God's revelations, blessing yourself, others, your mind, body, and affairs. Keep telling your mind that it is alert, keen, and clear. Affirm strength, vitality, health, and harmony in your body. As the centurion petitioned Jesus, "but only say the word." If you put the consciousness in the word (because words are only symbols), you draw from the breath of the Almighty.

The fourth and last step in creative communication is to find contact beyond the human role you play, and the role that everyone else seems to be acting out. Appearances will often tend to discourage your speaking the Word, which will seem lifeless at times just as does fertile seed lying in the soil. The farmer cultivates the seed, and we must cultivate our consciousness to nourish and cherish ideas of truth.

Consciousness communicates, thoughts broadcast; and our concern should be to express from the divine within, the spiritual center, to the circumference of our entire human existence. Communication is best expressed heart to heart. This was the principle Jesus relied on and testified to, a principle that every man can rely on through prayer, listening within for instruction and revelation in the "I-Thou" consciousness. " For I have not spoken on my own authority; the Father who sent me has himself given me commandment what to say and what to speak. And I know that this commandment is eternal life. What I say, therefore, I say as the Father has bidden me."

COMMUNICATION GAP

This statement cuts to the core of making sense: "Say what you mean, and mean what you say."

Metaphysical teachers may be inclined to think this phrase applies only to theologians; and I rather suspect theologians have equal reason to feel the reverse.

Language in religion, where theology and metaphysics share the same arena, can become confusing and complicated. Whatever direction thought takes, it takes the man with it. A teacher or minister often becomes mentally and emotionally involved with the value of words, terms, and phrases which his listeners are used to juggling in a purely verbal atmosphere.

"Say what you mean, and mean what you say" is given a great deal of assistance through an understanding of semantics.

No words can make metaphysical sense if they do not communicate spiritual thought in a simple, beautiful, meaningful, and moving expression. Truth literature and teachings dating back to the *Upanishads* and other early scriptural writings of Christian or pre-Christian origin have met this test to survive time and change. The poets, the sages of all ages, the saints, philosophers, and inspired writers throughout history have made metaphysical sense by knowing Truth and knowing how to communicate to all mankind. They expressed metaphysical sense before the term metaphysics gained prominence.

We must understand the real meaning of words without getting hung up on expressions that are just sophisticated, opinionated, or pious. The pitfalls in our verbal life have been well defined by Dr. S.I. Hayakawa, a foremost authority on semantics.

In writing on this very special subject, Dr. Hayakawa points out that *how* we apply words directly determines the outcome of our lives. He calls the application of words, "operationalism," by which we give the right or wrong meaning to what we say or intend to say. As an example, Hitler deliberately used the term "Jew" in a degrading way toward an entire race of people. It was his "operationalism" as a demagogue. Today the word "Jew" is used in a demeaning way by those who also harbor prejudice.

In the social and political upheaval of today, extremism of thought on the left and right subscribes to an operational vocabulary that does not meet the standards of brotherhood. It takes on subtle connotations which creep into the consciousness of the general public. The operational use of words in certain specific terms can incite riots, suppress freedom, promote the causes of war, or simply irritate a person to the point of anger, hurt feelings, and frustration. It all begins at home as parents know, and increases when a child enters school.

I believe metaphysicans and theologians should use words that promote mutual acceptance and understanding whenever possible. The very same principle of operational vocabulary can serve a creative and good purpose between any divergent groups.

We recognize, however, that certain words, though spelled alike, have absolutely different connotations. The interpretations, say, of "salvation" can never be one and the same. Reference to it is not the exclusive property of the fundamentalists; for the metaphysician believes that no one is ever separated from God. Therefore, he defines salvation as "not a thing, not an end, but a way."

It is a term we should not avoid because of its historic orthodox reference. We should know its definition from a total context of fundamentalism, and the metaphysical interpretation as well. If we shun certain words because of what others think, or of what we think we should think, language loses its savor and we reduce our inventory of words, our vocabulary, to a meager form of communication.

The Bible offers us good literature for making sense. The backwoods evangelist or metaphysical lecturer can build lessons about the same verse, allegory, parable, or text. Using a different dialect of understanding they measure out their messages according to the size of the cup the human mind can offer.

Animals communicate through simple, easily identified sounds, so they have their language. Alfred North Whitehead, a brilliant mathematician and philosopher said, "Spoken language is merely a series of squeaks." The animal has a definite sound for mating, warning, and distress call; an unmistakable and uncomplicated communication for every natural need.

Man, however, expounds at great length and gets very involved in speaking because he thinks deeply, and is treading water in the sea of his personal emotions, opinions, and attitudes.

I am not suggesting that we revert to animal sounds for simplicity of operational language; but neither should we return to the primitive level of communication used by our remote ancestors. Language evolved so man could make more sense man to man. Making sense from a public platform, at school, at work, in a social gathering, or over the dining room table involves us all in semantics. Our words heal or hurt, uplift or depress, harmonize or bring discord; opening our mouths to speak is a great responsibility in living. We clothe our thoughts in words, which has a parallel with the saying, "A man is known by the clothes he wears!"

How often contemporary words get out of hand, like "communist," "rightist," "conservative," "liberal," "radical" in political reference. The same is true in religion. A "fundamentalist" and a "traditionalist" are not all the things we may think in using such terms, because the individual is always *himself*. To speak to the individual and make sense is the key to understanding.

I think of myself as a metaphysician; yet I do not espouse every "metaphysician's" interpretation of life and God. I continually stress that fundamental Truth is the foundation of religion and metaphysics. Why? Because God is God! Truth has not changed through the centuries just because language has changed and new terms and terminology tend to confuse and complicate the verbal world of today. There is no need to shun the simple, direct, beautiful, and meaningful use of words because human involvement seems deeper than yesterday.

Is there a better way to say, "I love you," or "You are my friend," or "Let me help you"? We can strive to make our communication with each other operational in areas of agreement. We can succeed by using agreeable words. Insisting upon being understood *only* in our own terms or terminology constitutes the greatest verbal error of all.

Nothing is gained by being troubled because someone asks you if you are saved. You might disturb that same person by insisting that he believes in a myth when he holds to a literal acceptance of a Bible story. People get upset with each other over their differing verbal worlds in their Bible understanding. Certainly, there is no point in calling your questioner naive or dragging out differences sufficient to start another religious war. There is a wonderful proverb by Solomon that reads: "A word fitly spoken is like apples of gold in pictures of silver."

My wife's cousin in Canada paid the way for his brother to come from Poland and visit him. Later he visited us in the United States. He is a Franciscan monk and a Polish national, who was permitted to leave the country during the time a few years back when pressure on the Catholic Church was eased by the government there.

He told us that he was imprisoned with a Baptist and

a Jehovah's Witness follower during a time of religious oppression on the part of the Communist government. They shared true ecumenism in the same cell, and theology was not an obstacle to their feeling of spiritual kinship.

Words can separate us more than rituals. Knowing this, we can all work on our application of language, making it operational to heal, harmonize, uplift, and relate us one to another as brothers in the same world.

Metaphysicians are steeped in terms often alien to more traditional orthodox Christians. We should take great care to make metaphysical sense and not hesitate to speak of salvation, soul, or sin; but give their connotations in terms of modern knowledge. Our purpose should be to bridge the language barrier and beware of detours of pseudo intellectualism.

All religious belief gets its strength from an inner feeling that is intelligible in the heart of the believer. "A good man out of the good treasure of his heart bringeth forth that which is good . . . ."

YOU KNOW YOU CAN DO IT

If you are like me and most everyone else, there are times in your life when you find it difficult to get started to do something you want to do and should do. I am not speaking of common procrastination, of deliberately putting off until tomorrow and the day after that in a repeating pattern. I refer instead to that lack of confidence and will to do which keeps us precariously balanced in a state of inaction, torn between the desire and the doubt. Our indecisive, uncertain self is the problem.

My method for dealing with this human weakness is not a secret and certainly not profound. Just the same, it may as well be a secret if it is not brought to mind so that the "start button" of living can be resolutely pushed. I recall this method when a doubt beclouds a desire and prompts me to do something a little beyond my normal doing and my usual range of accomplishment. Coming to this crossroad, familiar to all of us, which for me is quite often, I simply tell myself, "You know you can do it." Then I repeat this affirmatively. I give my spoken word time. Sure enough, I hear wih deeper conviction the spiritual reassurance come back from the Spirit within me . . . "You *know you can* do it!" At this point my desire transcends all doubt, and I begin to take those first steps such

87

as a crawler learns to walk by or to make the noble effort such as a research experimenter makes that eventually brings him success.

This lesson in living was unforgettably dramatized for me many years ago when I was in my late teens. I had, at that time, adopted an elderly couple by way of an unusual relationship. This came about through a church contact while I was on a Good Samaritan project that involved me in their lives.

Every evening I would stop by their home to bank their coal fire and look in on them. The warm-hearted, motherly woman with whom I shared a mutual affection often made a pot of coffee while I was there. She and her invalid husband and I would happily converse together at the kitchen table as we drank coffee and ate sweet cakes so proudly offered on their meager budget.

One evening Mr. G—— (so I will call him) went through his usual ritual in going to bed first. He had an advanced condition of palsy, but he was always able to muster his will power and seize the right moment of reflex to quickly stand up from his chair and jerkily walk to the banister at the bottom of the staircase. There he invariably lost his initiative, being tired and uncertain as he clung to the support for balance. He soon renewed his effort, as if by some deep inner knowing, and his aroused spirit moved his body up the stairs with miraculous dexterity and timing. On the momentum of his courageous start, he moved like a robot wound up or charged with just enough power to cover the distance required. The whole process repeated at the head of the stairs, where he clutched the banister on the landing until he could spurt down the hall and into his bedroom. By that time I had said my good-bye to Mr. G——, and she would join him and help him in her own loving way.

One night Mr. G—— hesitated too long at the bottom of the staircase. Unable any longer to bear the sight of him standing there so helplessly, and with a sense of compassion, I went over to him and picked him up in my arms and carried him to his room. He was surprisingly heavy for a small man, strangely muscular from the unceasing shaking of his body. In those days I was an amateur weight lifter and very strong. Perhaps, in my teen-age innocence, I was unconsciously showing off as well as being kindly motivated. As I came downstairs, Mrs G—— caught my eye with a look of concern, rather than approval.

The very next evening that I visited these dear people, Mr. G—— almost reenacted the scene of the previous night. There he stood at the foot of the stairs, standing helplessly for what seemed to be an agonizing eternity. He looked to me with an unmistakable appeal, and I moved toward him to carry him upstairs.

Before I could touch him, Mrs. G—— called him by his first name in a sharp, scolding tone, as would a mother her child. "Benny," she said, "You should be ashamed of yourself, letting that boy do for you what you can do for yourself." Then, in a softer voice, which betrayed her deeper feeling and innate wisdom, she assured him, "You know you can do it." And he did!

Inwardly feeling guilty for having literally taken the problem into my own hands before, I had retreated. At the moment I was an outsider, but I understood there was no other way. Were I to carry Mr. G—— upstairs each time he seemed paralyzed, he would soon lose the small advantage he had to start at all. His problem, I have seen with reflection through the years since, was the same as we all experience at our point of challenge, only his was contained in his physical condition. What we each can do and must do is relative to our personalities, conditions, and circumstances. It is getting started that poses the great challenge of winning the day.

Many years have passed since I learned my great lesson. My two dear friends have passed on and attained, I am sure, a new and happier relationship. And here, I must use my method to win the day. Sometimes I struggle against all the reasons that seem to emerge from my unconsciousness to erect barriers to a desire that calls for my exceeding myself. Sometimes I think, as did Paul when he wrote the Romans, "For the good which I would I do not." How wonderful that just a little reminder can bridge this chasm of doubt and throw the balance on the side of doing what one must do, can do, and should do.

Try this method. Memorize these words, "You know you can do it." If you take this to heart as a workable truth, rather than a new idea, and repeat the truth for yourself, you will hear the voice of encouragement from the center of your soul echo back, "You *know you can* do it!"

There is a "start button," and you can push it. But you can push it only for yourself or encourage another person to push his own. Confidence is lost if living is done for us. We are the doers, and whatever the bridge to cross or the mountain to climb, it is best we face our own challenge. How can a challenge ever be unfair when "You know you can do it" to win the day?

A LITTLE GIFT FOR YOU

The heart in its wisdom can easily make words flow with an eloquence and simplicity that move the souls of those who truly hear. One need not be a professional to express sublime feeling and excellence of thought. Too much intellect in speaking of spiritual things can fail to communicate at a higher level of consciousness.

Some years ago I received a message from the heart of a woman who had patterned her life in accord with Unity teachings. It communicated magnificently. Her opening comment was, "This little gift is to commemorate my fifty years in Unity."

Only recently, coming across this woman's message in reviewing my personal papers, I came to realize "this little gift" was intended for you, the reader of this magazine. It was not written in the first person to me; it bears no salutation. It is the testimonial of one person's faith and inner feeling and it was only entrusted to my care. I kept it over the years because I became attached to the graciousness of her testimony and how it embodied the character of her belief.

Before I deliver "this little gift," you should know something about her. I first met her when she was a hospital patient and was recovering from an operation. She had a serene smile, stately bearing, and engaging countenance. Being inwardly poised and centered in a peaceful spirit, she had no need for reassurance about health. Her need seemed to be to talk about Truth ideas and the spiritual life. This we did, and I was pleased to become personally acquainted with her.

Over the years that followed, this very dear woman made occasional contact with me by telephone or letter. Sometimes it was a prayer request for herself or others, other times just a friendly note of appreciation. I would see her after Sunday services for a brief moment in the reception line. It always seemed to me that we would exchange an inner knowing, a continuation of our reaffirmation of Truth from that first meeting. She had, I knew, human problems, but she never surrendered her serenity or lost her *I am content* smile. Then I was told of her passing and was called upon to speak words of faith, comfort, and blessing.

The subject of this article typifies so many wonderful Unity women who have lived and are living Spirit-filled lives and I feel a special tribute is due them. I think of the many women over the years who have looked me in the eye and proudly declared, "I've been in Unity more than fifty years." I think of the early years when the teachers and ministers of Unity were mostly women. Unity's background of growth in the field ministry is unique compared with traditional denominations of America. One thing is certain, man or woman, bearing witness to ways of Spirit and treasuring the ideals that endure is sure to change the world and others.

In Truth we find a deeper accord of relationship. The reader and the writer are capable of equal understanding. The teacher is also a student and a student can become a teacher. When the wisdom of the heart speaks, words flow with an eloquence and simplicity that carry authority. One must always be listening for the voice of Truth, expecting it no less than a long-awaited phone call. Truth often speaks when we relax our searching for revelation, using for its voice the heart filled to overflowing.

Now it is time to deliver "this little gift" to you. I suspect she knew all along that I would eventually get around
to sharing it with you.

A Little Gift

"This little gift is to commemorate my fifty years in
Unity.

"In all those years God has never failed me although I
have failed Him many times. During those years I have at
times reached the heights of consciousness where I knew I
and the Father were one and could actually feel His presence a living thing within me. Yet in those years I also
experienced the frustrations of sadness and failure in the
valley of despair when I let the human self get in the way
of God's divine plan.

"I have known and experienced the great power of
God's love within me and the miracles it can perform—not
our little puny human love which mouths words of love
and goodwill but the great overwhelming love that flows
from God to us and through us. It is only as it passes
through us bestowing great impersonal love on everything
and everybody that it becomes an all-powerful magnet
drawing all good to us. Even God's love if we dam it up
inside us is powerless. Only as we let it flow through does
it become powerful even as electricity through the dynamo.

"I have found in those years that my obligations are
to God for His continued unlimited goodness to me. I
meet these obligations by keeping the high watch and
seeing in everything and everybody only the good He has
created.

"I have learned where to use the power of the will.
Even if we could, we have no right to use our willpower to
coerce other people. The power of the will is to be kept
at home, to be used on ourselves to keep us thinking and
seeing the Truth in all people, conditions, and circumstances no matter what appearance.

"I learned by painful experience that in Truth one

does not amputate but that when things are turned over to the Father completely, without reservation, everything is adjusted in divine order without hurt or harm to anyone and to the satisfaction of all.

"I think perhaps the most wondrous thing I have learned in these fifty years is that in true prayer, no matter what it is we are praying for or about, we come to the great realization that the Giver is always greater than the gift."

BLESS AND BE BLESSED

Some years ago I made a hospital call to see a man who had barely survived a second heart operation. He had been on the critical list a day or two before I visited him. After leaving his bedside, I met his wife in the corridor, where she had been waiting to see me privately. She was in a state of emotional distress, so we went to the lounge at the end of the hall in order to talk more freely.

Mrs. M—— had great faith and usually had a good outlook on everything, but her sensitive nature had been penetrated by a deep hurt. It seems the surgeon had been unable to give her any assurance regarding her husband's future progress. She felt that he had rebuffed her questions with a professionaly cold manner that lacked compassion.

I found it hard to believe, as I heard her pass judgment, that a leading heart specialist in a major city, who was much in demand, could be lacking empathy in the degree she expressed. But experience has shown that there is often misunderstanding and incomplete communication where emergency operations are performed and that time does not always permit treating the anxiety and loving concern of one closest to the patient. In my mind it just had to be a situation where professional posture was not equal to the fear and helplessness during this crisis.

As she unburdened herself of pent-up feelings, Mrs. M—— relaxed a bit. I could see that she felt a little guilty over her outburst, but she insisted the doctor had shown no evidence of compassion and had been abrupt with her on two occasions when she had persistently questioned him. This was not a happy situation, and I sought instant inner guidance to meet her need.

The thought I gave Mrs. M—— was very simple and a well-known remedy for Truth students. I asked her to behold the Christ in the doctor and to release any resentment or judgment. She was not convinced at first, but I patiently explained: "This man has great demands placed upon him. He has developed a professional manner; and when you pressed him for answers he may not have had at the time, it put him on the defensive. If he did have some of the answers, he may have felt it was not the right time to tell you. His withholding of facts could have been meant only for good. Between now and when you see him again, see the Christ in him, and you will touch his spirit where human contact has failed." She accepted this and agreed that spiritual treatment was the only answer. She believed in prayer and I felt sure that her blessing the surgeon would bring peace of mind and release for her. I had never met the doctor and did not really know his personal temperament.

A few days after my hospital visit, I got a phone call from Mrs. M——. There was the ring of joy in her voice as she spoke: "You know," she said "I did bless the doctor— I truly beheld the Christ in him. And, do you know what? On my next visit to see my husband, he apologized for the fact that he had been unable to explain the operation to me in the short time available. He even said he was sorry if he had sounded abrupt. Then, as he left me, he held my hand a moment and said, 'God bless you, Mrs. M——.' "

There is a spiritual law working through us all. It is to bless and be blessed. When I see testimony of this law at work, I rejoice as though a great miracle was performed. Why is it still uncommon for the heart to bless in the name of Christ? In truth are we not all heart specialists?

THE NEXT LARGER CONTEXT

Some words possess dimension, having an expansive quality. *Context* is such a word. In its general usage, context suggests the order in which things go together, the framework within which they occur, exist, or can be understood. Every person's understanding has its own boundary of coherence and meaning. We grow in consciousness by going on to the next larger context of thought and realization. Becoming aware of the next larger context of life, we are, by the very nature of our being, impelled onward. There is always a higher plateau of consciousness to be reached, a deeper reality to experience.

A good teacher rarely grades a good student's work perfect, knowing that he must continually strive tward a higher goal. We learn our lessons and unfold in character only as we see the next larger context and allow more room for improvement. I recall how Dr. Herbert J. Hunt, late dean of Bible studies for Unity School of Christianity, kept his students mindful of this important truth. On one occasion in his class on the New Testament, he gave me a mark in the upper nineties. With his professional thoroughness reflecting a personal interest in every one of his students, he wrote on the back of my paper an objective, constructive, yet kind ciriticism. He had a way of evaluating the strong and weak points in a concise summary. But what I remember best is this last line of his commen-

tary: "All in all, you have done well. Now, 'go on to perfection'!"

Perfection is always calling us on to cross the boundary
line of limitation. When we do cross from here to there we
see that perfection still lies beyond, in the next higher
context. As we ascend the steps of the ladder to higher
levels of realization, we get a new scale of observation. Did
you know that the rope ladder with wooden steps, leading
up the mast of a sailing ship to a lookout point, is still
called "Jacob's ladder"? From a more commanding height
we get a clearer view and truer picture of what is ahead.
The larger our scale of observation, the better truth comes
into focus and the illusions and inconsistencies in our
former understanding dissolve.

True learning requires that we unlearn much in order
to reach the higher point of view. It often takes a dose of
humility and cleansing disillusionment to let go of the old
and embrace the new. Facts have only a fleeting reality of
dimension, condition, and circumstance. They tempt us to
see only in the lesser context in which they manifest to us.
In Biblical times the ordinary person thought his world to
be a flatland with a vaulted heaven above it, instead of a
global sphere in orbit around the sun, within a galaxy
floating in a universe of infinite galaxies. Today we accept
many things that in time will be stripped of illusions and
misconceptions. We are still discovering the next larger
context of our inner and outer worlds. That is why Jesus
cautioned, "Do not judge by appearance, but judge with
right judgment."

Every transitional growth experience poses contradic-
tions to the past. The psyche has to reorganize to adapt
itself for entering the next larger context. This may be a
new stage of life, a new state of consciousness, or a radical
move in our personal affairs and environment. Holding to
the Truth in every situation, we can make the right judg-
ments and adjust in a higher consciousness. It is said that
Walt Whitman, who was forever getting the universal outlook and had a cosmic appreciation of life, was criticized

for changing his mind and sharply replied: "Do I contradict myself? Very well, then, I contradict myself!"

Charles Fillmore made it clear on a number of occasions that he reserved the right to change his mind. If a student quoted to him something he had written some years earlier, he was likely to ask that person, "But what do you think?" Then he would explain that he did not wish to be bound to what he had understood or expressed in the past, affirming that he was continually in a stage of spiritual unfoldment. Coming into Truth (as it is often phrased) means getting a more universal viewpoint of life, self, and everything. In this repeated process of new birth we unfold into higher and higher states of consciousness.

The facts in our life constantly change, just as trousers become baggy and dresses wear out. Haven't we all at times felt that our thoughts were too baggy, or worn out? George Bernard Shaw once remarked that the only intelligent man he knew was his tailor, who would take a new measure of him every time he ordered a suit, never assuming that he was always the same George Bernard Shaw. In the same sense, a changed consciousness requires new dimensions of awareness to be properly clothed.

In the normal order of our affairs, questions come before answers. Asking the right question, inquiring beyond our present understanding, creates a magnetic affinity with the right answer. "Ask, and it will be given you" is proved when we move to the next larger context of understanding. This includes seeking to find and knocking on the right doors, those that open on inner chambers of Mind.

Exploring beyond the boundaries of the personal mind, keep asking yourself "What if?" Look at everyday situations with a new approach, from a higher point of view. Think of possibilities in every situation, and let your imagination soar. Then engineer it down to earth. All human progress comes from those who keep asking "What if?" Look at the larger context in yourself. Consciousness is your expanding universe, the kingdom without end.

Prophets and great souls of past and present have been a profound influence for good. It is said that they were "born before their time." This is misleading, because their greatness and power was the result of their seeing in a much higher context than the average person. Time does not prevent us from knowing higher truths; only our stage of consciousness makes the difference. Do you remember Mark Twain's satirical romance, "A Connecticut Yankee in King Arthur's Court"? It is a story of a nineteenth century Yankee who woke up suddenly in the court of medieval chivalry. With his shrewdness and knowledge of modern inventions, and his knowledge of an imminent eclipse of the sun that he predicted just before it happened, he gained great power and influence throughout the land. His awareness was in the next larger context, where the human race of that time had not yet arrived. But the true purpose of getting ahead in consciousness is not to pull the wool over the eyes of the natives, to exploit the naive, but to go on beyond the context of personal opinion and changing facts to see, as Paul stated, "what God has prepared for those who love him." Da Vinci, Edison, Einstein were products of their age who functioned in higher dismensions of mind than their contemporaries. Jesus, Buddha, and many of the great saints shared higher contexts of inner awareness as spiritual food for the multitudes of their generation and those to follow.

The Hindu mystical teaching has a beautiful word and concept of spiritual adoration . . . *darshan*. Darshan is an experience that brings one into a vision of light, and refers to the spiritual power and fortitude that emanate from a great soul, as with Mohandas Gandhi. The Hindu believer literally bathes in the presence and peace of one who is so recognized and divinely endowed. Who can deny that those living in the larger context of love, understanding, compassion, and faith can magnetically draw others into their greater field of spiritual affluence, being who they are and where they are in the consciousness of God?

What does it take for the seeker, the Truth student, to get to the "there" of the next larger context from the "here" of the present context? Yes, it takes affirmation, prayer, and meditation. And this must reflect in integrity of action, humility, and honesty with self. Like Walt Whitman, be unashamed of contradicitng yourself to embrace the rightness of spiritual principle and a new awakening. Like Charles Fillmore, reserve the right always to change your mind to accommodate your unfolding spiritual awareness. Be as practical as George Bernard Shaw's tailor, and keep on taking new measurements of yourself. If, all in all, you think you have done well, "go on to perfection." If you reach what was yesterday's destination, let it be a beginning for tomorrow. Go on to the next larger context, and the next, and the next.

Across the centuries the words of the prophet are still reminding us . . .

> "For my thoughts are not your
>   thoughts,
>   neither are your ways my
>   ways,
>   says the Lord.
> For as the heavens are higher
>   than the earth,
>   so are my ways higher than
>   your ways
> and my thoughts than your
>   thoughts"
>   *(Isaiah 55:8, 9).*

THE MAGIC TOUCH

The hand of man can do so much,
Possessing God's own magic touch.
From fingertip to mind above
There flows the current of His love.

In a moment's warm handclasp
A friend is found within one's
grasp.
And gentle hands, without speaking,
Console the heart while yet out-
reaching.

God ministers through you and me
To unify humanity.
We need but follow love's command
To find His magic touch at hand.

NOT WITHOUT LOVE

With a spirit both tender and tough
I can deal now with "life in the
rough";
A gentle hand here, a firm hand
there,
And lots and lots of love to spare!

YOU CAN BE FREE

You can be free,
    And all the joys of heaven find,
God lets you be
    What you believe in heart and mind.

God keeps you free
    By His grace of sweet forgiving.
That inner key
    To heaven is in prayerful living.

Take heart, and rise
    Beyond the shadows of your mind.
Press on! The prize
    Is yours when doubts are left behind.

You will be free!—
    When faith, heart, and mind combine
To inwardly
    Embrace His infinite design.

MEDITATION

God is love. God's love teaches me to love with the constancy, wisdom and acceptance of the love implanted in my heart. My soul is touched by the revelation given to Jeremiah: "I have loved you with an everlasting love." I let God's love flow as the unifying, healing, harmonizing power of my life. The universal and magnetic field of Love holds me to Its virtue and uplifts me to express a higher degree of empathy, forgiveness. kindness, understanding, and soul-to-soul affection.

"Love is not love which alters when it alteration finds." These words of Shakespeare remind me to stand fast in my love. I will let the inner flow of love flow outward and rise supreme over personality and negation. Love's magnetic field cannot be broken by human deviation and indifference. I will know as Paul affirmed, "Love bears all things, believes all things, hopes all things, endures all things. Love never ends." In this knowing I will be wise, decisive, firm and fearless in dealing with adversities, yet with a nonresistant spirit I will let love have Its way. "Perfect love casts out fear."

As the virtue of true love blooms in my soul, I will trust its invisible and indivisible power. I will build upon divine affection. Love beats in the pulse of my heart. Love's acceptance is electric in my handshake. By the power of God's love I will deepen my affinity with others, loved ones, all creation. May my love be worthy so that God's love is not impeded by any human reservation to love freely on my part. In my way, I seek in every way to love with an everlasting love. In loving as I am already loved, I would that others find the peace of mind love has given me.

105

IV

**INSIGHTS FOR AFFIRMATIVE AND
CREATIVE LIVING**

THE DYNAMICS OF AFFIRMATION

Dynamics has to do with forces that produce or govern activity of any kind, and the methods of such activity. Affirmations demonstrate by the law of dynamics because they can inspire, motivate, and initiate changes in one's mind, body, and affairs. Charles Fillmore believed (and proved) that the right affirmation, used with understanding and faith, can get things going for good in any area of man's life. In his book *Atom Smashing Power of Mind*, he explains the power of affirmative thought in this way:

"We say 'strong as steel.' But a very little thought will convince us that mental affirmations are far stronger than the strongest visible thing in the world. The reason for this is that visible things lack livingness. They are not linked with energy and intelligence as are words. Words charged with power and intelligence increase with use, while material things decrease."

One of the most popular and dynamic affirmations was prescribed by Emile Coué, a druggist who left medicine to practice his own unique method of healing psychology. At his clinic in the city of Nancy, France, he developed the method known as Couéism. Using the dynamics of affirmation and encouraging patients to use their power of autosuggestion, he got remarkable results and hundreds of testimonials. Some Americans went to him for treatment, and he eventually crossed the Atlantic for a lecture tour, successfully spreading his healing psychology to thousands. That was back in the Twenties, when society, intoxicated with many new ideas ushering in changes in living, was ready for a positive self-help technique.

The affirmation he popularized still lingers on in the memory of many people today: "Every day in every way, I am getting better and better!" This was Coué's basic prescription, and he recommended that one should repeat this a number of times in the morning on getting up, and again at night before going to sleep. The idea was to get one's subconsciousness to accept completely this declaration. His genius was his ability to "put over" the idea to be affirmed and get people to use their natural power of autosuggestion. He claimed no miracles, saying simply: "I do not heal people. I teach them to cure themselves."

Affirmations do "work" when they are dynamic in their phrasing and the dynamics of their use is applied. But we believe that the power goes deeper than that of autosuggestion. Spiritual power is freely given to us from the Christ Mind within. It is as Paul affirmed so dynamically in his letter to the Philippians: "I can do all things in him [Christ] who strengthens me." Even so, the subconsciousness must get the message and respond. Faith with feeling is the key to the subconscious resource of energy and intelligence at your command.

The Christ Mind responds when man calls forth the inner qualities and potential inherent in his spiritual nature. This calling forth from within is really the naming power. The generic term given for man in the Bible is Adam. Adam possesses the power to name things for God, for his own highest good. "And whatever the man called every living creature, that was its name." To name for God means to affirm for good. Unfortunately, if one experiences negative feelings he may affirm a negative. This warns us to watch our feelings so the dynamic power is not misdirected.

All affirmations should be statements of truth. Our ideal is to name everything for God, for our highest good.

This role poses a very great responsibility, for as it is written in Proverbs, "Death and life are in the power of the tongue." The tongue is only an extension of a person's thoughts. If we are to watch our tongue, we must first watch our inmost thoughts. Our everyday dialogue with others, even the constant soliloquy within ourself, commits us to what we affirm. Words are linked with energy and intelligence, which we tranform into manifest results in all areas of our life.

I have seen how many of the affirmations that appear in leaflets, books, or periodicals have had truly miraculous influence upon people. The statements that bring the best results are usually more dynamic in their wording. The wording itself is important in getting through to the heart and mind. We need to be inspired, stimulated, and the right words at the right time act as a powerful lever in our consciousness. Among many Unity favorites, here is a good example: "Divine order is now established in my mind, body, and affairs." Why is this dynamic? It is to the point, and it covers everything and anything. It calls for total expectation.

Emile Coué offered good advice when he recommended that self-treatment be the first and last thing in one's conscious hours each day. In the morning an affirmation is effective because the mind is fresh and what one decrees is said with enthusiasm and vitality; it is a beneficial influence throughout the rest of the day. In the evening an affirmation has a different advantage. It is well known that the last thing we hold in mind before we lose outer consciousness tends to penetrate our subconscious activity like oil injected into a rusty lock. This is like sending a child off to school with a happy thought. If you scold and nag the child, you cast a negative shadow on his day. Likewise, the last thing said between a husband and wife on their parting in the morning has great influence on their outlook throughout the day. So give the subconscious mind a good thought on retiring, a blessing for your total well-being as you surrender to your inner consciousness.

A good, dynamic thought can marshal all the dynamic powers of the soul to victory while you sleep.

Have fun with affirmations. Work with different ones that appeal to you and your need. Write out an affirmation especially for yourself, in the spirit of "to me, with love." Keep the one you are working with at the breakfast table; stick it to the mirror you look into when you first rise. Keep one on the night table by your bed, or on your bureau. Develop the dynamics of affirmation in your life as a good habit rather than a strict mental discipline. Your subconscious mind relaxes when you relax, and then it is most receptive to command.

You are a dynamic person, simply because you are a spiritual creation. Watch your feelings. Watch your thoughts. Watch your tongue. Use the Word of God, through your words, with imagination and boldness. You are still in your Adamic role, naming things in the creative unfoldment of life.

> "You will decide on a matter and it will be
> established for you,
> and light will shine on your ways."

BE MASTER OF THE MOMENT

Now is the most important moment in your life! This has always been true since man was first conscious of time. The present moment is a state of being—the eternal now. When we think of the past or the future we establish different states of consciousness. We could not be in the states of Missouri, Washington, and Texas all at the same time without being physically disunited. Neither can we split our conscious thought into three states of mental activity without losing the greater power of concentration. To do so could be compared to the legs of a centipede suddenly going in three different directions. By instinct the centipede walks in a Divinely ordered way. Not always man! He is free to go the way of his thoughts. Otherwise, he could not find spiritual growth in the individuality of his consciousness.

Successful businessmen realize the importance of mastering the moment, and do so to the degree that they apply the right principles of living. The following story illustrates this point:

Several years ago I held a key position as head of a department and responsible to an extremely busy and successful executive. He was confronted each day with so many phone calls, interviews, and letters demanding his time and decision that it would appear he faced the humanly impossible. I had been in his office to discuss various problems requiring his decision. Incoming phone calls competing for his time constantly interrupted our discussion of the matters at hand. He calmly and carefully made notes of every conversation. I suddenly became aware that he dealt with more detail and petty annoyances than I or any other member of his staff.

He finally called the switchboard operator and put a temporary halt to the phone calls so we could complete our discussion more easily. Just before leaving his office, I surprised myself by blurting out, "How do you ever keep on top of everything?"

Gesturing toward a huge stack of papers on his desk, he smiled and replied matter-of-factly, "Oh, I just work from the top of this pile and do first things first."

He continued to explain that he first delegated all the work he possibly could to his staff, leaving only notes from phone conversations, reports, and letters that he could not release from his personal handling. These he stacked on his desk, with business requiring immediate attention filed on top and future business toward the bottom of the pile. Each day he handled the current business, starting from the top of this assorted pile of papers. Thus, he always worked the pile down to the next day's business before he left the office each afternoon. I remember him looking me squarely in the eye, after telling me all this, and saying, "It never fails to happen. Things of tomorrow take care of themselves better than I can settle them today."

This man admitted that in earlier years he had tried to solve problems prematurely, but he was beset by fears, worries, and insomnia until he learned the hard way to do first things first and let tomorrow take care of itself. He had learned to sleep at nights without conjuring up nightmares about what might happen the next day, next week, or next month. He had discovered that the challenge of the moment required all his power of concentration. We might say of him and other successful businessmen who search inwardly for the right principles of good business, "There is a spirit in man: and the inspiration of the Almighty giveth [him] understanding."

Since that day, I have thought many times how Jesus answered this all-important question of how a man can live free from these distracting cares and worries: "Take therefore no thought for the morrow; for the morrow shall take thought for the things of itself. Sufficient unto the day is the evil thereof." It seemed so simple, do first things first and "the things of tomorrow take care of themselves." Jesus and this executive were two thousand years apart in stating this one truth, and their personalities are equally distant to each other. The wisdom of their words, phrased so much alike, is more than coincidence. It proves there is a spirit of truth active in the heart of every man, the principle of right action, that unfailingly illumines the mind that seeks a better way.

The fearful attitude of "What will I do tomorrow" soon causes confusion and disorder in our lives and affairs. In desperation man turns to God. How much better it is to find the answer through the resourceful and positive action of a prayerful mind before a problem reduces us to despair! How much better it is to consciously master each moment!

What is it, then, to do first things first? How do we keep from thinking of yesterday's failures and of tomorrow's dire predictions, free to concentrate upon the present day's work and do it the right way? It is done by living in the eternal now, mastering the challenge of each moment. We can succeed far beyond our highest expectation by affirming a mental attitude that consciously declares, "I am the master of the moment. I meet the challenge of the moment successfully."

The Apostle Paul said: "This one thing I do . . ." And with this approach he pioneered the conversion of the Gentile world of his time so successfully that he might be called the greatest salesman Christianity ever had in the field. He faced his world prayerfully, with an attitude of mind that concentrated all his mental powers upon meeting the challenge of the moment.

When we direct all our efforts and thoughts toward mastering the moment, each moment as it comes, our future success is assured. A mind centered in God is concentrated upon the very spirit of mastery within each one of us. Regular, affirmative prayer soon brings this realization.

Robert Jones Burdette wrote: "There are two days in the week about which and upon which I never worry. Two carefree days, kept sacredly free from fear and apprehension. One of these days is Yesterday . . . and the other is Tomorrow." Tomorrow is but an expansion of today. Divine order assures us that the unfailing truth, the principle of right action in business and in living, always leads to success. I have found greater meaning in life and richer rewards every time I have truly faced the challenge of the moment. So many distractions are encountered in today's fast-moving business world that it is good to remind ourselves of "This one thing I do." Prayer is the best state of mind in which to decide the bigger problems of the day. Regular prayer establishes the prayerful mind that will master the moment and take the right action on all problems, big or small. Spiritual mastery is a practical approach to living and working. It is your true state of being in the eternal now. "Now is the accepted time!"

TIME IS OUR RESPONSIBILITY

My position fits into the broad category known as "junior executive." As a buyer for a large wholesale grocery firm, I am exposed to pressure and tensions in a fast-moving, highly detailed, and competitive business. My occupational surroundings comprise mechanized warehouse operations, click-clacking machines in the office, and the eternal hubub from processing orders, setting up new sales promotions, interviewing salesmen, reflecting on market changes, and facing an onslaught of new items that appear faster than we can discontinue old items.

For seven years I labored diligently in this atmosphere, and perhaps I was too eager to surpass my co-workers. Each year I assumed more and more responsibility and work. The work load overflowed into the comparative serenity of my family life. Every evening I arrived home just in time to sit at the supper table—tired, and with at least one stockbook and detailed material that required attention. It got worse each year, until the situation became almost intolerable.

Patience and love on the part of my wife prevented any emotional conflict, but the amount of work I kept bringing home was a problem we discussed at great length. Helen pointed out that I seemed unable to regulate my work load during the working hours at the office and that I was intensifying the problem by allowing it to become a

116

chronic habit. I had to agree with her. It finally became clear to me that I was actually stealing time from my family and the problem was mine to solve.

As I look back now, I can see that it never should have become a problem. Unfortunately, thousands of men are caught in this situation simply because they have not learned how to apply moderation within the competitive race of worldly activities. Perhaps they have sought the answer to their dilemma within the limitations of their personal ambition rather than consulting inner Spirit to see if they are expressing God's design for progress. This was true in my case. However, such a fault ultimately leads us to realize that our faith and spiritual soundness are just as much a part of our occupations as they are of our personal and private lives. Running into a blind alley can be the turning point for finding the main road.

To me, heartfelt thoughts are prayer: moments when I meditate alone, whether I am driving a car, sitting in a chair at late evening, or in some manner seeking the counsel of God by expressing a will for a good outcome in something that deeply disturbs me. It was at such a time that I found the answer in the guise of a parable.

I have a six-year-old son who, typical of his age, has no sense of time. One evening, after finishing two hours' work at home, I watched him as he got in bed and quickly fell asleep, exhausted. He played the game of life so hard that he pitted all his energy against time itself; he needed direction and training, so that the power within him could be harnessed for a creative and wholesome future. Being a father, I could see that and love him for his enthusiasm; despite the lack of restraint in his play, I knew that experience and counsel from me would help him to mature soundly. I had faith that he would learn to control this power within his mind and body. Then I realized that I too am a son—a son of God.

My first act was to tell my wife that I was going to adjust my life so that work hours did not overflow into our home. I assured her that no matter how busy I was at work, I now realized that it was within my power to rearrange the affairs of my life in a harmonious pattern. I knew that only good could result if I did so with conviction.

The Monday following, I started my first week of what I good-naturedly called my "austerity program." This consisted of half-hour lunches, no coffee breaks, and starting work an hour earlier each morning to finish any business left over from the previous afternoon. There was no home work, and I was home each evening in time for supper. I did not put off necessary work or allow my new work schedule to interfere with the service I owed to my firm.

At the start of the third week, I prepared a memorandum to my immediate superior in which I set forth the actual working hours required for me to perform the duties and responsibilities of my position. The length of my working day was impressive, inasmuch as I noted the shortness of my lunch hours and sacrifice of coffee periods, which alone gave me five hours of extra time weekly. My memorandum, written in a straightforward and friendly manner, explained how I had taken home more and more work throughout the years until it became a real problem. It stated that despite the work load of my job, no one had ever instructed me to take work home or expected it of me. I did not, however, minimize the amount of work required of me or the demands it made upon me to do a conscientious and efficient job.

My closing words were: "Inasmuch as I am sure management is aware that some reorganization and additional staff or clerical personnel for the buying department is needed and will be unavoidable as operational plans are progressing, there is no need for me to intrude with comments beyond my personal situation. My intent here is to state factually a condition that exists. One problem, that of taking work home, I have ended myself. Of course, were an emergency to keep me here for forty-eight hours, I would stay gladly."

After allowing the boss time to read and digest this resolution, I saw him in his office to assure him that I was devoted to my work and was not complaining. I admitted that I had caused the entire problem by taking work home in the first place. Then I reminded him that I had asked for some relief in the past and I felt that this account of my time clearly set forth my needs, which previously could not be fully evaluated because I was in effect working overtime each day by taking the overload home.

He expressed his appreciation of everything I told him, and I left his office without pressing for any answer. The full weight of my announcement had left him slightly abashed and I knew he would act when and as he saw fit.

Within a few weeks we added a new secretary in the buying department. The new worker proved highly capable and took on quite a few duties and responsibilities that I was able to delegate to her. Other changes made within our operation made it possible for a new department to take some of the buying off my hands. The management made it clear that our reorganization and increased staff should equalize everyone's work load to a point of efficiency and to everyone's satisfaction. A much closer spirit of cooperation was established as a result of this.

My time is my responsibility. It is a definite asset. The company I work for owns a large block of this asset, and I own a goodly share of it myself. I am not the victim of time, of my work, or of anyone's whim or dictate. In the great design for living, just the opposite is true. Having devoted myself to my job, expending and expanding my talents toward a creative end, all within the limits of a well-planned and scheduled day, I can produce more work of high quality.

I believe the alarming number of nervous breakdowns, heart attacks, ulcers, and many "occupational disorders" that thrive on worry and fear are due to error in our thinking and deafness to God's will. Time is a measure of life: it tells us when to stop this activity and start another. In this concept I am happy in every effort I undertake. I welcome each day with a fresh outlook and find decisions easy to make. If a problem is too big for me I can get spiritual guidance for the asking.

Life is not a marathon race. We set our own pace. Time runs for us, not against us. After all, it is our responsibility.

IT'S YOUR MOVE

The society in which we live does not always encourage brotherhood, the true fellowship we seek to enjoy and share. We should face the fact that we are responsible for our relations with others.

Several years ago an incident helped change my outlook on this problem. I received a birthday card from a salesman who had called on me only once or twice and would normally be known as a "brushing acquaintance." Despite the fact that our relations had been all business, he had remembered this important anniversary in my life. Such a thing had never happened to me before. It seemed more than a thoughtful gesture.

The next time the salesman called at my office I thanked him and asked him how he ever got the idea of sending birthday cards to casual business acquaintances. His straightforward answer was:

"Well, all you fellows are grown men. I know myself how little your birthdays are remembered now that you are grown up. It seemed to me that this was the least I could do, and everyone I send a card to seems to get real pleasure out of it. I've been doing it for years."

This man never sought any favors in my consideration of items he offered for sale. I usually had to turn down products he offered. But he knew that the most hard-headed businessman would appreciate a thoughtful greeting card.

That birthday card I received inspired me to write to ailing business associates and fellow workers to cheer them and extend my prayers for their well-being. I have found that this develops mutual respect and understanding. This is true whether I write to a boss, an assistant, a competitor, or somebody else.

This world of increasing luxury, conveniences, and material progress exposes us to the temptation of receiving without giving. We cannot escape moral laws by indifference or inaction, however. Sometimes when things seem to be going well in this fast-moving and functional operation called the business world, the lack of something will bring spiritual discomfort within the very depths of our being. This is our hunger for a spiritual identity.

Progress in our business growth is a result of discovery and research; it must be good, and inseparable from God's design for tomorrow. Inspiration has built the largest corporation and drawn the blueprint for the most complicated machinery. The same inspiration that created giant industry and big business will conceive and create universal brotherhood. What should awe us about the growth of industry and business is the miracle of the spirit behind it all that urges us on, that inspires us to find our identity with the good.

How do we apply moral intent in a world where we may feel our role to be minor and insignificant? Herein is the challenge, to use our soul force and express ourselves with free choice. We must first of all stop taking things for granted. Material gains can usurp our initiative, deaden our true desires, and destroy our identity, unless we assume mastery over negative conditions. Our attitude should affirm that God has a divine plan expressed by truth and love. Every phase of life must be evaluated according to its potential good.

Competition should not be regarded as a deadly struggle. Instead, we should appraise the diversity of services and products as an advantage in achieving success. We should cease thinking that we are competing with our fellow workers for position and prestige. In truth we are working with others to create more abundance for mankind's better standard of living. This goal should be pursued with peaceful ambition and positive belief in our own success. Such an approach will bring us an everlasting fellowship to bless our relations with everyone with whom we have daily contact.

In business today there are many examples of Christian priniciples working to lift society to the level of worldwide fellowship. Some large corporations practice tithing; many firms share scarce materials with competitors. I know of a fast-growing chain of independent grocers who advertise jointly under one name. Whenever a new store joins their group or one of their members expands into a group or one of their members expands into a second outlet, these grocers pool available personnel from all corners of the county and send some of them to work at the new store during opening week, without cost to the store.

Each year "Good Neighbor" drives throughout the nation are expertly directed by high-salaried executives who donate their time and talents with the blessing of their own firms. No less important, people at every level of society contribute to these charitable fund-raising activities that have been our accepted responsibility in helping the less fortunate ones among us.

Look about you; see the need to express Christianity in every word, thought, and action. There is no time to take things for granted. Your identity on the job is important. It is your move to greet others with conviction when you say "Good morning," especially to those who take the day for granted.

THE DOOR SWINGS BOTH WAYS

In the search for spiritual realization great emphasis is put on going within, meditating, becoming still, entering the "inner chamber." There is no doubt that the door to God swings inward. No one really knows the Father's will, gets divine direction, unless he turns his mind inward to the Source.

What is often overlooked is the two-way swinging action of the door to Spirit. Practical Christianity teaches that we go within so that we may express the will of God to the highest glory of mankind on the perimeter of life— the out-here-and-now stage of our human existence.

William James, the American philosopher, once recalled a childhood experience that dramatizes what could only be illustrated through the innocent observation of a child. He remembered writing (while still a child) to a friend about a summer home his family had acquired in New Hampshire. He was quite excited about it at the time. In his letter he wrote, "It's a wonderful house, with all the doors opening outward."

We must go within to find and stay on the spiritual path. This is true; but this is for inspiration and direction. The road of life offers us no fulfillment on the way unless our mind opens outward, our heart opens outward, our interests open outward. Jesus taught a sequel to His teaching of going within: "What you hear whispered, proclaim upon the housetops." This is literally what we do when we bear witness to the Truth. In this "swinging world" we must remember that the door to Spirit swings both ways. A door that leads only into oneself is not what the Divine Architect designed. Wherever the waters do not mingle and find an outlet, there are dead seas.

THE CREATIVE VOID

These past ten years I have saved a newspaper reprint of comments taken from an article written by the late Dag Hammarskjold. This great man, a celebrated mystic among statesmen, was awarded the Nobel Peace Prize in 1961, a year after his death. The particular item in my files is revealing of his spiritual philosophy as related to the wide range of variance in men's belief about God. He stated: "One of Buddha's scripts states that the significance of the vessel is not in the shell but the void. In other words the significance of a room is not the walls but is in what is framed by the walls."

At the time I read this, the words of the second verse in the first chapter of the Book of Genesis came to mind. "The earth was without form and void; and darkness was upon the face of the deep; and the Spirit of God was moving over the face of the waters." The allegory suggests, one might conclude, a creative void in which we can project the essence of our faith to demonstrate a new spirit, a way of believing that transcends all religious forms. In the creative process creative activity never ends using the fluidity of ideas, potential forms, as the Spirit moves "over the face of the waters."

The reason Dag Hammarskjold spoke then of the void or emptiness of the shell was to explain why a small space, reserved for a meditation room at the United Nations Center, was furnished with no altar (in the conventional meaning of that term). It had, instead, only a block of iron ore placed in the center of the room where light from above could strike it in a descending shaft and set it glimmering like illumined ice. The stone thereby became an altar to the God of all, and provided a sanctuary that respected all religious symbols among the many member nations with their diverse cultures and differing faiths. To Hammarskjold it symbolized that the United Nations was dedicated to turning swords into plowshares. It represented the idea that God gives us the basic materials of life, and we shape of them what we will. It all depends upon our having the imagination to see the creative void and use our spiritual powers for peace and progress.

We easily get carried away with symbols, old forms, the appearances of our individual beliefs. This blinds us to the challenge of always filling the void with creative activity. The Bible tells us, in allegorical style, how the Creator creates through the void, moving "over the face of the waters" (formless, seed ideas of Being), to bring forth the master Plan and infinitely express Itself. We too in the formlessness or seeming void of mind can think creatively without being bound to the vessel or shell, the old form. With every other man, we can find a common faith-foundation on which to stand free of restrictive symbols and religious patterns that have served their purpose. The ultimate world community church must be a universal awareness with no sectarian bias. And, I believe, the higher worship that will unite us all will be established and is now being founded in the creative void, where the individual spirit alone must work free and unbounded by symbolism that is archaic.

When I hear the words of some of the "new" music my sixteen-year-old daughter plays on her stereo, I sense the stirring of a new religious awakening. This music recommends spiritual love, becoming as a child in the sense Jesus taught, living in peace and attaining peace of mind. It is not to be confused with the wild, shouting, lusty, unintelligible types of some modern recordings. But make no mistake, the divine discs are being cut, and they are being played by the jovial jockeys. As with all Truth, you must listen carefully or you may not hear the message. The emerging new generation wants to merge all kinds of faith and religious practices as one. Even behind the Iron Curtain contemporary lyrics of love, peace, and brotherhood capture the attention of the youth who are ready to enter the void for creative living.

In reflecting upon this statement, "the significance of the vessel is not in the shell but the void," I recall a favorite quotation from the sermons of the great fourteenth-century mystic, Meister Eckhart, whose teachings were pure metaphysics. He said, "The shell must be cracked apart if what is in it is to come out; for if you want the kernel, you must break the shell." You see, we cannot stay with all the soul gathers to itself, apart from life unfolding everywhere. Jesus taught the same when He said, "Unless a grain of wheat falls into the earth and dies, it remains alone; but if it dies, it bears much fruit." That is the creative process, life always filling the void.

The challenge in the religious world today is for us all to get out of our ecclesiastical casts and put our best foot forward, to march to a more sublime tune and keep in step. In the orderly death of old forms, restrictive symbolism, the spiritual life of mankind is raised higher. We need only declare the void good, and move fearlessly and faithfully into it.

IDEA POWER

One good idea is all you need
to begin a demonstration.
It only takes one seed
to produce a new creation.

MEDITATION

I see myself as a creative spiritual being, conceived to be a perfect expression of God. I know that God in me cannot fail or lack for anything. Omnipresent Spirit sustains me in the wholeness of life. Omniscient Mind illumines me, guides me to right decision, inspires me to original endeavor. Omnipotent Power fills me with strengthening life and endless energy. The One Spirit is always accessible to renew my faith, deepen my understanding, and fulfill my heart's true desires.

Day by day I dedicate myself to express what is best for my health, happiness, growth and success. I know my own will come to me. I sow and reap with a free spirit, in absolute trust that there is a divine law of supply and demand. God is my partner in business, my counselor in prayer, my inexhaustible resource for creative ideas. I work from my divine center to the outer circumference of human affairs. My inner and outer life serve each other in perfect accord.

I give thanks that living demands spiritual growth. I rejoice for all that is entrusted to my care. My desire is to share rather than to possess what the universal storehouse provides. I seek to serve, even as I am served. Spirit prospers me in my sharing and serving. Assured of continual divine supply, I covet nothing yet dare to claim all I can manage and consume. "Eye hath not seen, nor ear heard, neither have entered into the heart of man, the things which God hath prepared for them that love him." (I Corinthians 2:9)

The wellspring of living water fills my heart to abundance, "I shall not want." My cup truly runs over, and I am grateful!

— from INSPIRATION FROM THE INNER "I"
by Norman V. Olsson

V
INSIGHTS OF PHYSICS AND METAPHYSICS

THE POWER OF A FRACTION

Charles Fillmore was a man with a penetrating inner vision. His prophetic writing and profound teaching harmonize spiritual principles with the most advanced scientific knowledge. He often theorized in areas of thought where later discoveries proved him correct.

In one of his books, he expressed the conclusion that "the vital energy of eternal life exists in every cell of our body." As long as sixty years ago, he expounded on the omniscience, omnipotence, and omnipresence of God in the cells and atoms of our bodies. In *Christian Healing* he made this observation: "Physical science has discovered every atom has substance, force, and intelligence; these are the three constituent parts of mind." It is clear that he recognized the wholeness of life in its microscopic fractions and realized that the power of a fraction is the power of the whole.

Charles Fillmore's teaching stressed man's transforming power of thought through the right exercise of free will. He taught how right thinking regenerates the cells and atoms of the body when one claims his inherent spiritual power and perfection as a son of God. He perceived that these fractions of life were divine units of "substance, force, and intelligence." They respond to the very direction of our faith, joyous attitude, love and praise. Worship is reverence for one's own life as well as the life of others, a continual affirmation of our creation in the image and after the likeness of God. Such pure thought activity in-

132

fluences and excites the cells and atoms of the body to manifest their highest unity of expression.

One obvious illustration of the transforming power of thought is a person's capacity to blush. A fleeting blush stirs our atoms and produces a chemical action in our cells. Illness or healing comes through the activity of atoms and cells. Extensive studies into psychosomatic illness prove the unhealthy effects of negative thinking. But increasing interest and study in the wide field of spiritual healing testifies equally to the regenerative power of right thought, prayer, and meditation. True spiritual treatment unifies the fractions of the perfect whole.

The principles of both mathematics and metaphysics are expressed through absolute action of exact law. Good thoughts add their blessing, negative thoughts detract or subtract, inspired thoughts multiply through wonderful realizations of Truth, and confused thoughts divide. Our demonstrations are the net result of the total activity within our consciousness. Plato, one of the greatest thinkers of all time, was quoted as saying that "God is a geometrician." Current research and discoveries in the study of atomic and cellular life support this statement, only to deepen our conviction that creation is founded on perfect order and perfect patterns. God is at once the supreme Architect, unfailing Principle, loving Father, Source of all. It is literally true, as Paul told the Anthenians at Mars' Hill, "In him we live and move and have our being."

As a geometrician, God is eternally original. Your fingerprint identifies you alone when compared to the fingerprints of millions of other people. Of the trillions of snowflakes that fall each season, no two are ever shaped exactly the same. Perhaps this is what William Blake alluded to in his immortal verse:
"To see a world in a grain of sand
And a Heaven in a wild flower,
Hold Infinity in the palm of your hand
And Eternity in an hour."
The point is that the whole is in the fraction, and the

fraction is in the whole. Life is more meaningful and promising when you feel that you have a grip on infinity, and can see the opportunities of eternity beyond the limited awareness of what you must do in the next hour.

Just recently some experimenters at Oxford University transplanted an ordinary body cell from a frog's intestine into a fertile frog's egg. It would not seem logical that reproduction would result from a tissue cell—but it did! The discovery was reported in a newspaper that I read.

Oddly-Made Frogs

One plain frog body cell, transplanted into a frog's egg, can grow into a complete frog, say Oxford University experimenters.

The wonder of this discovery is not the shortcut to reproduction without sex, but the nearly unbelievable "genetic coding" contained in just any old cell's tiny nucleus.

One intestine cell, embedded in egg cytoplasm, suddenly "knows" how to duplicate and grow such specialized cells as brain, eye, skin, glands and everything else a frog needs to be a frog. There is more information programmed within a little dab of frog meat than in any giant computer.

Doesn't this substantiate Charles Fillmore's statement of a generation ago that "the vital energy of eternal life exists in every cell of our body"? In terms of our computer culture and electronic age, we might say that God has "programmed" Himself into every cell and atom. Every fraction contains the potential omniscience, omnipotence, and omnipresence of the Creator.

Even though we may not see outwardly the whole scheme of life or comprehend the perfect whole of Spirit, we can always work with the power of the fraction through believing, trusting, accepting the whole Spirit. Jesus taught that the power of faith can perform wonders when it is only "as a grain of mustard seed." He expanded this metaphor and explained how consciousness can be cultivated and developed into the awareness of the whole spiritual realm, the kingdom of God. "[It] is like a grain of mustard seed which a man took and sowed in his field [mind]; . . . when it has grown it is the greatest of shrubs and becomes a tree, so that the birds of the air come and make nests in its branches." Is not the symbology clear? Use the power of the fraction to find the whole equation of health, prosperity, friendship, life, the fulfillment desired.

Thoughts are fractions, yet each righteous thought calls forth the whole of what it represents in itself. The seed of thought is precious, powerful, and filled with promise. The poet can "see a world in a grain of sand." You can see God in a single thought. It is given us to use the power of the fraction. "Now I know in part; then I shall understand fully, even as I have been fully understood."

PROGRAMMED FOR PERFECTION

All functions of life in their natural order are divinely programmed toward maintaining and perpetuating an inherent idea of perfection. Even the chemistry of the microscopic single cell is designed upon principles of self-generating, self-renewing, self-cleansing action. Order and balance are the natural state of things, and the appearance of new life is readily recognizable by its glow of perfection. If the inherent glory of creation does not always find its fulfillment within one life span, it is not because the programming is faulty. Man by his excesses and extremes has disturbed and disorganized natural order to the point that today he fears pollution as greatly as he fears war, famine, and epidemic disease. This fear has precipitated an increased interest in the science of ecology and has forced man to take steps to "clean his environmental house."

When Jesus instructed us to "Consider the lilies of the field, how they grow," He gave us a perfect example of divine order at work in nature. A simple blade of grass is so common that we hardly notice it, and yet it silently works to fulfill our great need for pure air. Receiving little recognition for its service, the green shoot removes polluting gases from the air and returns pure oxygen. A well-maintained lawn measuring fifty by fifty feet produces enough oxygen day by day to meet the needs of a family of four. Green vegetation is programmed to carry on photosynthesis, and each blade of grass uses the energy of the sun to turn carbon dioxide, water, and minerals into green growth and purifies the air in the process.

God, the divine Intelligence, the universal order that is immanent in all creation, has programmed the blade of grass, the single cell, the tiny, invisible atom, and the giant, glimmering galaxy by means of immutable laws. His central plan perpetuates a cohesive cosmic unity. Everything is divinely "computerized" for a good and perfect unfoldment. We see the evidence of God's handiwork all around us. Just as a well-kept garden tells us that a wise and careful gardener is at work, so the order of the universe tells us that God is in charge.

From the spiritual point of view, it is both comforting and reassuring to know that all creation is programmed for perfection. The earthworm enriches the soil. The star's exploding nova contributes somehow to the galactic equilibrium. In man's own case, a Sufi mystic has written:

"I died a mineral, and became a plant.
I died a plant and rose an animal.
I died an animal and I was a man.
Why should I fear? When was I less by dying?
Yet once more I shall die as man, to soar
With blessed angels, but from angelhood
I must pass on. All except God perishes.
When I have sacrificed my angel soul,
I shall become that which no mind conceived."

Too often in metaphysical teaching the word *death* is considered an anathema. Death should not be called "God's will," but can be seen merely as a change, an opportunity for transmutation, transformation, transcendence. Death is the means by which the program for perfection provides a new beginning, a new birth, a renewed entity of expression. Jesus was referring to this process of rebirth when He said, "Truly, truly, I say to you, unless a grain of wheat falls into the earth and dies, it remains alone; but if it dies, it bears much fruit." As his spiritual awareness expanded, Paul found that his mortal consciousness decreased: "It is no longer I who live, but Christ who lives in me."

Although man has allowed war, famine, and pollution to wreak havoc in his world, he is finally beginning to realize that he can no longer ignore the innate perfection of creation. It has become evident that ignorance and disregard for the laws of conservation bring definite negative results. At last man is showing real desire and effort to achieve spiritual unity and to establish a higher order on earth. A trend toward increased reverence for life and understanding of God's cosmic will is evident in the world. The people and the powers of the world are beginning to perceive the meaning of Jesus' words, "Not my will, but thine, be done."

Emerson had a particularly enlightening way of expressing the deeper facets of spiritual reality. He wrote: "All our progress is an unfolding, like the vegetable bud. You have first an instinct, then an opinion, then a knowledge, as the plant has root, bud, and fruit. Trust the instinct to the end, though you can render no reason." Life soon enough gives man a reason to be good, to respect nature, to love creation, and to revere in its true being all that is.

Some years ago a friend called me, frantic because her four-year-old son had swallowed nearly a whole bottle of aspirin. The ingestion of such an amount of the drug could have had fatal or highly damaging effects. My friend had gotten immediate medical assistance and then called me for spiritual help and prayer. Hearing her appeal, I searched for guidance in offering the right affirmation. In a flash the words came to me, and I said in a calm tone of voice: "Trust the chemistry of God. We know that the chemistry of God is greater than the chemistry of man." She and I trusted. Within twenty-four hours the crisis had passed, and her son's body functions were balanced and normal. The order of life was demonstrated once again.

Sometimes we do not always find immediate solutions to our follies, accidents, and webs of human entanglement. But eventually all is brought to order, for all history has been a progression forward and creation continues to unfold. This unfoldment is programmed into all life. Perfection is God's goal through us, for us. The blade of grass teaches us to refine the worst of our environment and give it back as a pure expression of life. Nothing happens without meaning to the total scheme of things. Jesus said of the sparrow, "And not one of them will fall to the ground without your Father's will." There is a perpetual continuity to the rising consciousness in every form of being. The child in us is transformed into adulthood through the struggle of our teen years. Middle age prepares us to slow down, to mellow, and to live a more meditative life. In our later years, we gain a spiritual vitality as we proceed, phase by phase, according to the natural order of spiritual growth. To trust the program for perfection is to say, "My Father is working still, and I am working." Wherever our cooperation is lacking we see problems, encounter negative conditions, and reach difficult crossroads.The evidence of error carries with it realization of the Truth to follow. History has shown repeatedly that man and nations can take a right turn when necessary and overnight dissipate a threatening catastrophe.

We do not question why a flower must risk exposure to the elements, the vagaries of the growth process, and the uncertainty of survival preceding the final bloom. The blossom is so perfect that it erases all doubt, reverses all judgment, answers all questions. The method and the means hardly exist between cause and effect. In our present consciousness, we are too aware of the pain of birth and of the seeming finality of death. We must not forget the joy of new birth; we must see death as a release making possible receipt of more life. Is it not enough that we are programmed for perfection? "But if God so clothes the grass of the field, which today is alive and tomorrow is thrown into the oven, will he not much more clothe you . . .?"

YOUR INNER GYROSCOPE

Do you remember the toy gyroscope (it seems to have disappeared from toy departments today)? For sheer wonder, it was about the most scientific and demonstrable a device a child could play with. I recall one I had as a child: of simple but very precise construction, an inner steel wheel that could be spun on its axis inside an outer spherical frame that remained stationary. Once the wheel was set spinning by quickly unwinding a tightly wrapped thread or string from its hub, the entire gadget, frame and all, would stand upright with a tiny footing on the rim of a glass or a taut wire. Top-heavy of itself, the gyroscope obeys the law of its action, known as "gyroscopic inertia" or "rigidity in space." Even a toy top, which is a more top-heavy object demonstrates the gyroscopic principle in motion. As you know, a top's stability while spinning is such that it will often right itself if knocked over while it is still whirling.

Now consider how your thoughts revolve around a central preoccupation or idea. Thoughts seem to rotate about whatever your mind is centered upon. This ability to hold to a stabilizing center in consciousness suggests the principle of an "inner gyroscope" maintaining one's mental balance. In Biblical language, the maximum benefit of this thinking principle is recommended in Isaiah:

"Thou dost keep him in perfect peace,
whose mind is stayed on thee."

Truth students interpret this to mean "holding to the Truth."

There are moments when anyone may feel mentally lopsided, top-heavy; and one in such a state of mind may say, "I feel as though I am walking on a fine line." Interestingly enough, he may be balancing himself mentally on one good thought or strengthening affirmation. Stability founded on one sustaining thought is the result of our "inner gyroscope" at work. As the true thought lifts one up in consciousness, a greater stability brings about peace and poise. Man can literally think himself into a sphere of healing, harmonizing, spiritual activity. Unity has for years recommended a powerful affirmation that has helped thousands find the freeing influence of the Christ Mind:

"I am poised and centered in the Christ Mind, and nothing can disturb the calm peace of my soul."

Charles Fillmore once explained that "the personal self is the ego around which revolve all thoughts that bind us to error." It is a paradox that the ego of itself provides a temporary center about which the gyroscopic action of thought maintains some degree of stability. But the ego-centered mind suffers as its axis of preoccupation keeps shifting. Real stability is found only in a God-centered mind, just as the earth keeps uniform seasons and perfect equilibrium by revolving on a true axis. Were the axis of the earth to change, as has happened in ages past, our entire globe would undergo chaotic changes until a new axis was established. That is why we should avoid the lesser gravity and unstable center brought on by fears, anxieties, and negative preoccupation, striving always to fix our consciousness in the greater sphere of spiritual thought.

We must remember, too, that preoccupation with self excludes others. Our thoughts, to maintain real success and stability in living, must gravitate about the unity of all life, the inner and outer man, husband and wife, family, society, mankind, and God indwelling all.

There is a misconception about thinking which suggests that too much thought activity can bring on mental breakdown, confusion, and the like. This is not true! Thinking of the gyroscope again, consider the turning wheel. A wheel in motion will establish greater gyroscopic inertia, or balance and stability, the faster it turns. If you are driving on a turnpike at seventy miles and hour, under the right conditions you can be more relaxed than if you were going ten miles an hour with a flat tire. The friction or stress has to do with a broken circle of action rather than with the acceleration of motion or thought. You cannot master riding a bicycle until you attain sufficient speed to keep your balance. Just sitting motionless on the bike, you are top-heavy and will fall down unless you plant your feet on the ground. It is the symmetrical action of the wheels above a minimum speed which counterbalances the force of gravity and sustains your position.

In the celestial mechanics of our universe, order is maintained by gyroscopic action, "rigidity in space," so the stars and planets can spin or stay fixed in their respective positions as they follow a charted course in the seeming void. And there are the spiritual mechanics of mind, principles of thought, which bring us into many spheres of consciousness in this great wheel of life. It is as Jesus said, "In my Father's house are many rooms; if it were not so, would I have told you that I go to prepare a place for you?" Each sphere of awareness has its own degree of stability, depending upon the size of the orbit you consciously travel. Universal thought survives influences and events that might throw intensely personal thought off its course. In the universe the influence of the greater body is always dominant. In consciousness the influence of the Christ Mind represents the greater power and presence of God in man, as his divine and only true center.

Large ocean liners use a gyroscopic device by which a

compass shows true north, unaffected by the magnetic pole. A supersensitive gyroscope is used as part of the controls for automatic flight in supersonic aircraft and guided missiles. Every self-guiding system requires stability. We, in the complexity of our thinking-emotional nature, should trust the "inner gyroscope" so providently built into our very being. The forward-moving, balanced, spiritually-activated thought keeps us stable. In the orbit of spiritual thought we have an unerring guidance system, divine direction, for reaching our goals and staying on course.

You feel your head spinning only in the smaller orbit of consciousness, when you are mentally bound to the personal center. At such a time, affirm: *"I am poised and centered in the Christ Mind, and nothing can disturb the calm peace of my soul."* Do this quietly. It is the best remedy you can prescribe for yourself.

One illustration in metaphysical teaching points out that an individual centered in God-awareness is as safe and secure as an airplane pilot in the perfect calm of the eye of a hurricane. That is to say, in the midst of negative forces, physical or mental, you can find peace, protection, and stability in a God-centered consciousness. Your "inner gyroscope" offers both guidance and security as you lift up your thoughts to the higher spiritual spheres.

THE WORLD IS GOING METAPHYSICAL

Surely you have heard the expression, "the tides of our times." It stresses how new ideas, new trends, new fashions happen everywhere with epidemic porportion the moment they take hold. This truth is more clearly seen if one traces back the origin of great inventions. Radio, television, and nuclear energy were being researched and perfected almost simultaneously on both sides of the Atlantic.

Several European countries claim invention of the automobile, the radio, and other great discoveries as products of their research. In some cases several men share the distinction of developing the same idea, yet they lived and worked unknown to one another. In fact, in perfecting the automobile Henry Ford was considered a latecomer who had simply "gotten in on the act" and capitalized on a "hot idea."

Another phenomenon of universal coincidence is seen in the building of pyramids. These huge triangular structures were built as tombs both in Egypt and Central America three thousand years ago, with neither civilization being even remotely aware of the other's existence. A great deal known in the Mayan civilization matches the evolution of science concurrent in the history of Egypt and Asia Minor. Rather than speculate on vague theories that ideas were transported by a daring voyager, we can give credit to the divine Intelligence uplifting and inspiring man wherever he had his primitive earthly beginning. It is as Victor Hugo confirmed in his famous declaration, "There is nothing quite so powerful in the world as an idea whose time has come."

Today we are witnessing new "tides of our times." The world is going metaphysical. Although metaphysicians have been around as long as the oldest sciences and arts, metaphysical study has only been popular and exposed widely to the public during this last century. The very word *metaphysics*, and everything properly classified as metaphysical writing and teaching, belong to our time as never before. *Metaphysical* literally means that which transcends the apparent, visible world we experience with our outer senses. Jesus was a metaphysician and He established the principle upon which metaphysical thought is founded when He taught, "Do not judge by appearances, but judge with righteous judgment."

All religion dealing with the inner life and the development of spiritual perception is by this standard metaphysical. The difference today is that religion is expressing more and more meaning and application as mature metaphysical thought replaces myths, superstitions, dogma, and shallow piety. The religious instinct in man is a great motivating force. It is so active in the contemporary world that tidal waves of spiritual activity are washing away old, outworn traditions. Man is seeing the need to subordinate everything in his physical-existence awareness to higher considerations. The Stone Age, the Iron Age, and the Atomic Age were all progressive steps on this material plane propelling man toward a Spiritual Age. Evolution, human progress, and advancement result from the stirring in the soul of that one Spirit working through us all.

My writing this article was inspired by two incidents in my life within a span of two days. First, I found a young man in his late twenties with whom I could converse with an equal exchange of metaphysical thought at a very high level. He said he had "arrived" at his realization through his scientific inquiries that sparked the fire of soul-searching. Intensive intellectual inquiry raised questions he could satisfy only by a spiritual awakening, a transcending of the intellectual consciousness. He personified in my eyes the beginning of what is happening to young people all over the world. I have had many "rap sessions" with young people, enough to see which way they are going—and which way they will take the world with them.

The second significant incident was the surprise of seeing portions of a book by an outstanding metaphysician reprinted in the weekly news and business journal, U.S. News and World Report. The editor had devoted the entire back page to it—space that was reserved for editorial comments. The reprint was titled "A Key to Happiness." Though it may have seemed out of context, it was timely and pertinent to the reader's need. It was published, I am sure, because the whole world is beginning to go metaphysical.

Just forty years ago a metaphysical movement known as Seicho-No-Ie got under way. It claims over two million followers. Where is all this growth for a new religion? In Japan, the land of Shintoism and Buddhism. Why? Because the world is going metaphysical

The modern metaphysical movement got off first base just about a century ago. The spiritual principles being introduced at that time in America were also being taught by independent schools and in publications throughout western Europe and Great Britain. Modest as the pioneering work was, it represented a concerted start under the direction of the one Spirit inspiring men everywhere, whose time had arrived. (It might better be said "by men and women," because many outstanding metaphysicians who led the movement were brilliant, inspired women.)

Our young people, here and abroad, are giving public testimony to beautiful and pure ideas in their songs and through convictions of practical idealism. They feel with a depth not fully appreciated by those who harp on the drug cult and revolutionary extremism. If we will give the new generation a chance, just half a chance, they will show us the pattern for a better world.

When my daughter recently graduated from high school, I heard an honor student address his peers, dignitaries, and family members present with a message of spiritual common sense which echoed such strength of conviction that the auditorium became a sanctuary of hope. He received the greatest applause among the speakers, leaving an impression his elders could not match. One board official tried, in the terms of our younger generation, to "down" him. But this only weakened the official's own stature and displayed a contrast of verbal futility. We all wanted to be "upped."

Like so many of my generation, I am apprehensive of all the upheaval, destruction, and discord associated with our times. But when I get quiet, meditate, and reflect on it all, there comes an assurance from within that life is only regrouping, reorganizing, renewing its forces for a great spiritual breakthrough. These tidal waves of change moderate to a gentle, cleansing surf action by the time they touch the shoreline of our personal life. What is happening everywhere at once is divine design rather than human accident. Whereas the metaphysicians of the past, ancient wise men, were voices in the wilderness, now Truth is gaining a voice everywhere—in business, in the press, in educational institutions, in the home, in the hearts of men and women who "hunger and thirst after righteousness."

I bless the young people who cry out against war, pollution, hypocrisy, and whatever denies the freedom of spirit. It is time for us all to get away from the subjectiveness of metaphysical thought and objectify what we have revealed inwardly by, to paraphrase the gospel, "shouting it from the rooftops." Man must transcend his problems, his limited nature, his very incompleteness on this plane. Such a great miracle is conceived in metaphysical thought, but the thought requires the right words and deeds. A new appreciation of life is needed. We need the feeling of the refrain sung by the late beloved "Satchmo," Louis Armstrong: "What a wonderful world! Yes, I think to myself what a wonderful world!"

SEEING LIFE IN ITS TRUE LIGHT

Thanks to Sir Isaac Newton, science discovered that outer forms or things have no color of self. It is the refraction of light rays moving through their atomic and molecular structures at 186,000 miles per second that infuses them with the qualities of the cosmic spectrum. An autumn leaf has no color in darkness, but the same leaf changes color with subtle variation in relation to different degrees and intensity of light from dawn through high noon to dusk. Light is the great transforming agent.

An analogy can be made with respect to the inner light being refracted through the structure and character of our thoughts that characterize the individual consciousness. Jesus reminded us that we should be mindful of how we reflect the inner light when He said, "You are the light of the world." Sunlight can only manifest as much color as a prism will reflect. Consciousness is a prism for Divine Mind. Spiritual qualities and attributes are revealed according to one's personal consciousness.

Thomas Masson, one of America's more outstanding journalists of recent years, wrote considerably in the field of metaphysics. He expressed the opinion that "the spiritualization of thought is the only thing which can save any one of us." Once an editor of Life magazine, associate

149

editor of the Saturday Evening Post, and known as a brilliant intellectual, he became a free-lance writer in later years and devoted himself to absolute truths. He told a true story in his experience which I believe portrays the ineffable reality of seeing life in its true light.

A woman friend showed Masson a photograph taken when she was eighteen years of age and which revealed the face of a most beautiful young girl. At that time, his friend happened to be over forty. Another friend in their company gazed at the photograph also and quickly exclaimed, "How much more beautiful you are now than you were then!" The woman who was showing the photograph of herself in her radiant and photogenic teens replied, "How can you possibly say that when I am now so much older and certainly more faded, and even beginning to be wrinkled?"

Thomas Masson, in recalling the incident, said he felt that at the time this woman was more beautiful. Her face had taken on light in the intervening years that was not reflected in her countenance when she was so much younger. There is a quality Spirit can reflect through one's consciousness that is eternal and defies age and personal appearance.

There is "the true light that enlightens every man . . . coming into the world." The spectrum of all the divine attributes and ideas of the one Spirit is ours to reflect through the prism of consciousness. Nothing is more beautiful in nature or in another soul than to see life in its true light.

It has been said that a drunken man uses a lamppost for support, but a sober man uses it for illumination. Truth is not merely a support to hold us up. Truth is the light within, seeking every thought of man to release its imprisoned splendor to the world. Seeing life in its true light beautifies the person who sees with the single eye and lets his whole body be full of light. Beauty is not only in the eye of the beholder; it can *be* the beholder.

ATOMS AND STARS

Every atom has a heart,
And a part within each part;
A depth that reaches in as far
As the space-span to a star.

Inner-outer life can meet
Like two friends upon a street.
Be not misled by big and small—
Atoms split, and stars can fall.

Through the universe at night
Photons flow in steams of light.
Just as the wave and sea are one,
Every atom has its sun!

CELESTIAL GREETING

Somewhere there is another earth
Orbiting its star of birth;
An Eden of humanity
With its own society.

Somewhere another human face
Looks deep into depths of space,
Awed by the scintillating light
Other suns reflect at night.

The watched and watchers, eyes intense,
Share a common reverence;
Both send forth celestial greeting—
Prelude to time of meeting.

MEDITATION

I am one with the One Reality. All nature relates to my physical organism. All energy is the scintillating atomic light that embodies my soul. All intelligence is programmed into the very spirit of my being. My human form is created out of the dust of the earth, but my spirituality is the essence of God individualized in the self I am. The eternal breath of life, breathed into me from the very beginning of creation, assures my immortality.

My thought traverses the universe faster than the speed of light. My soul-awareness knows the depths of divinity. My faith entertains every probability of any given moment, and in its God-conscious heights of awareness accepts nothing as impossible. "With God all things are possible."

Free electrons and ageless atoms shape and reshape my finite form from the cosmic reach of infinity. I am divinely organized. In my manifest self the image and likeness of God unfolds with eternal persistence to be more perfectly personified. From the true vine I have branched forth to bear the fruit of my Christhood.

My finite personal self realizes that Absolute Principle governs the universe. In finite self is the Infinite Spirit! Its law is the order for the self-renewing phenomena of nature. It is observed and measured in the science of physics. At the cause-and-effect levels of life I evolve. In my inner consciousness of God's grace I am quickened to transcend former, lesser states "in the twinkling of an eye." My Divine "I" assures me I am a god in the making. It is written in the scriptures "you are gods." Let it be so!

153

VI
INSIGHTS OF TIME,
ETERNITY AND IDENTITY

ALL THE TIME YOU NEED

Would you like an eternal supply of a universal asset, something of infinite value that can never be depreciated or exhausted? Essentially, you already possess it in the dimension of your mind. Like anything of great worth, unless you manage it with responsible administration it is devalued by lack of appreciation. This preferred asset in the market of life is commonly called "time." It never runs out for those who learn to blend its measure meaningfully into the moments, days, months, years and seasons of their lives. The secret of all hereto said is held in the consciousness of our spiritual life. Charles Fillmore taught, "Time has no power over one who dwells in the mind of God."

Our present day pace of living may tend to give us a time complex about all we do, keeping tight schedules and organizing around the edict of the calendar. On a larger scale, Presidential candidates in an election year race back and forth across the nation meeting timetables the average person would consider impossible to keep. Less conspicuous and unheralded, a solitary, domestic worker near retirement age may be meeting the daily challenge of commuting to work each way by taking two buses, walking several city blocks, and maintaining a home where another member of the family, older and infirm, is lovingly cared for in those later hours of a long day. Somehow, each of us in the circumstances and roles of our lives learn to come to terms with time. We cannot ignore the schedules here on the human side, in the world, nor hold back the hands of a clock. A cynic may say that time is unkind. But viewed with a spritiual sense of appreciation, it can be said that time is the kindness of God, always there to be used and as fresh as our daily bread. We all have all the time we need.

There is a beautiful verse to be found in Paul's letter to the Ephesians, first chapter, "For he has made known us in all wisdom and insight the mystery of his will, according to his purpose which he set forth in Christ as a plan for the fullness of time, to unite all things in him, things in heaven and things on earth." To trust God is to trust in "the fullness of time." Paul uses this phrase in other references. It is a wonderful concept and standard to live by. Getting a true conviction of how to work with time is invaluable to one's peace of mind and understanding. Time is adaptable, as the writer of Ecclesiastes stated, "For everything there is a season, and a time for every matter under heaven."

A story is told about an Indian student riding in an auto with a modern speed demon. The driver of the car saw a train coming and said, "If I don't cross the tracks ahead of this train we will lose three minutes." He stepped on the gas and just made it across the tracks with only seconds to spare. When safely across, the Indian philosophically asked, "Now, what are you going to do with the three minutes?" In terms of reality, you can never gain or lose time. Time is best judged as to whether or not it is used wisely or unwisely. If used unwisely, then it is wisdom not to waste more time regretting or reviewing the dead past. Time is the raw substance of life and is always there to be shaped anew and woven into the character we give our moment-by-moment existence.

Unity stresses living in the now, the eternal now. In this respect, the student of Truth does not have to give too much preoccupation with past lives or karmic influence upon the future. God is with us every moment. The declaration of God identity still speaks as it did to Moses centuries ago, "I AM THAT I AM." Only this moment counts. One moment is a pearl strung on the necklace of eternity. When we master the moment we mold our own fate and insure the future according to the consciousness we demonstrate.

A free soul has developed a sense of timelessness and can meet schedules and maintain an organized life without being earthbound, weighted down by worldly affairs. We all know or observe outstanding individuals who have attained admirable self-control and mastery while deeply involved with great demands upon their time. Such a person seems to work and move about with a poise and command that affirms, "I have all the time I need." Jesus was never hurried. Account after account records how the disciples tried to pressure him to take action of one kind or another. Even the sisters of Lazarus, whom he loved, could not rush him to their aid to raise their brother from the dead. But he did it in "the fullness of time."

At home, at work, in familiar places or where one feels "out of his element," coming to terms with time determines happiness or unhappiness, success or failure, making friends or feeling friendless. The right attitude inspires creativity. Your mind is your time machine that can take you to the right state of awareness for dealing with any situation. Your freedom to use this universal asset of infinite value that can never be depleted is absolute. Acting with a sense of priority, spending every moment wisely, feeling God's purpose supporting your deepest desires assures that all things in heaven and on earth will unite for you in "the fullness of time." You have all the time you need. How are you using it?

THE ETERNITY FACTOR

If we knew life's reality in its entirety, we would know of the eternity factor. But for the most part, our awareness is only fractional, so we see the arc of the "now" and not the complete circle of our overall existence.

Nevertheless, the "now" *is* eternal if we penetrate it through faith, spiritual perception, and intuitive knowing: there it waits, absolute and timeless in itself, for our discovery. The well-known invitation to find it is stated in the Bible—"the kingdom of God is at hand"—assuring us that it is possible to step into eternity now!

One of the most mistaken of all beliefs is that of thinking eternity to be a futuristic dimension, something distant, beyond the threshold of time. However, time can be both illusive and deceiving, as Einstein proved in his theory of relativity. He would humorously explain how inconstant the time dimension is in relation to experience and states of consciousness, by saying, "When a man sits with a pretty girl for an hour, it seems like a minute—but let him sit on a hot stove for a minute and it's longer than any hour. That's relativity."

The fundamental precepts of metaphysics teach that God, the Power and Presence, is not focused in the past or the future. The past always merges into the present, while the present continually provides the opportunity for

shaping the pottery of things to be. Jesus reminded us that
it is within the individual's power of perception to see how
the fields are "white already to harvest," and he consis-
tently stressed a need for the *faith* to visualize present and
future in one context, always releasing the past. To the
thief on the cross, who was repentant and preparing to
accept full responsibility and judgment for his crimes,
Jesus spoke words of forgiveness and assured him freedom
and Divine pardon. "Verily, I say unto thee, today shalt
thou be with me in paradise." Is not this a far cry from
suggesting that there is some kind of a karmic sentence
which is unavoidable and must be served as a sort of pur-
gatory?

We all stand somewhere on the staircase of life. Looking back into suspected or believed-to-be previous lives,
we might see much of our future very heavily mortgaged
and ourselves indebted in many future lives just to satisfy
karmic law. On the other hand, we might wonder about
the "hereafter" and invite voices or contacts from "the
beyond," for some guarantee or evidence of how our
future life and affairs will turn out.

Either way can stir up our psychic nature to fantasize
unwittingly, perhaps to fabricate an answer that will
appease the soul's yearning, and while it is wonderful
for anyone to experience a spontaneous breakthrough
into spiritual knowledge and understanding, it should not
be forced. The Inner Spirit seems intuitively to guide us
to let the doors of perception open when we are ready to
enter, not allowing us to break impulsively through the
walls that separate the "many mansions" of other planes,
whatever they may be.

And yet, anyone who can ask the basic questions
about life wants to know more about the eternity factor.
Many souls, seeking the meaning of their existence and
hungering for spiritual identity, consider the whole gamut
of current speculation and belief. They look into the theory
of reincarnation, spiritualistic claims, out-of-body testi-
monies, reports of soul regression, and excursions into

higher planes of being. Their will to believe often excites a romantic response in the psyche and stimulates their imagination, with credence being given to whatever the human mind may conceive as possible. When they find a thread that keeps repeating, even a slim evidence of confirmation common to the great varieties of belief, another step into eternity may be taken, although the dilemma of mankind seems still to fit the description given by Paul when he said, "For now we see through a glass darkly," not yet "face-to-face."

The Christ within is the spirit of liberation that brings grace to the believing mind. Though we all have many steps yet to take on the spiral path into eternity for individual fulfillment, the beautiful enchantment and true romance of living with our ideals is likely to be dispelled if we keep counting every step and looking back to measure the way. What kings or queens could ascend a stairway with sureness of foot, majestic dignity, and perfect bearing if they looked down to check on their footing at each step, or searched back to see how they were being regarded by others? Many of our present life journeys to new horizons of living would have been aborted had we worried beforehand or questioned too closely the cost, the inconveniences, the many unresolved factors. Truth expresses best through a faith that never loses sight of its goal, a faith that is, moment by moment, expectant of unlimited good and perfect outcome here and now.

Although much is said about the beliefs of the people in Jesus' day and their acceptance of reincarnation as fact, Jesus in his ministry expressed the power of grace as being unconditioned by the Law. John understood this and made it clear when he wrote, "For the law was given by Moses, but grace and truth came by Jesus Christ." When our healing and help come in seemingly miraculous ways, as they often do, bringing us what we desire in "good measure, pressed down, shaken together, running over," the karmic spell is broken. And we must admit that a belief in grace works as well for the fundamentalist as it does for the person more metaphysically inclined, as it all has to do with whether or not one is willing to step into eternity now, in a spirit of faith. (Indeed, I often hear the phrase, "I am working out my karma." It is a statement of resignation, one void of inspiration. How much better it is to say and to believe, "I am rising above my karma.")

I have met many reformed alcoholics. (Though most of them disclaim being reformed because, I believe, they are fearful that such complacency will lower their guard against a regression to the former habit.) Some have made an overcoming in a year or less, after a period of complete addiction. Others have not found freedom before two, five, ten, twenty, or more years have passed, as the time factor seems to relate to when *they were ready* to demonstrate and reach out for a new level of consciousness, a realization of the personal freedom to act resolutely.

We break from the past and also (to be precise) the present, stepping into new states of eternity, the very instant we dare to see, to do, and to be what is our spiritual potential. Our potential self knows no time factor other than the eternal, and no one is chained to a karmic wheel. Anyone, by his own choice, can stop the replay of the music and hop off the merry-go-round. There may be details to be worked out, challenges to face, but the break can be made and is being made by individuals every day.

The theory of reincarnation can be significant for some in providing an answer to how Divine provision is made to give the soul ample opportunities to become fulfilled, though from a purely pragmatic point of view, one needs only to believe in the progression of the soul, in higher states of unfoldment, in the right to transcendence. But who can sort out the fact from the fiction, the real from the unreal, the truth from the fantasy? Paranormal happenings may be the byproducts of our spiritual, psychic, and physical forces intermingling, being out of joint, or both. Truth, however, does not rely upon the "unexplainable" or the so-called supernatural to be self-

evident. Truth is embodied in our lives *here and now*, in
the everyday context of living and in the larger dimensions of self-realization. The hands of the heart can touch
eternity and feel its ethereal character. And when we open
our spiritual eyes there is no confusing activity or bizarre
imagery to be encountered. Jesus reduced the qualities of
eternity to descriptive similies: "the kingdom of heaven is
like . . . ." While we theorize, research, and look down
every alley of belief, each step into eternity is only as sure
as our footing and the balance we finally achieve. Indeed,
the least sensational step may be the most forward one.

Wordsworth wrote, "The world is too much with us;
late and soon. Getting and spending, we lay waste our
powers." This suggests that, in our spiritual searching, we
should not strive so hard that we may actually block or
distort our powers of perception.

Eternity is synchronized with the "now." All Truth is
here. The doors of opportunity never close, and being alert
to the "Divine openings" in the realm of consciousness is
the joy and revelation to be found in prayer and meditation. When we see inner doors open, we should hold them
open with our faith and belief until our passage into a new
awareness is complete. The eternal reality and the limitless
good of God is not changed, for always "the kingdom of
God is at hand."

No matter what restrictive factors I may have faced at
my human level of existence in the relative world, I have
always had the freedom to think the most sublime thoughts
along with those shallow and mundane ones. All of the
great religions have stressed the virtues of thinking sublime thoughts, for the eternal virtues of love, peace, order,
forgivenesss, and patience do not fail. Neither do the ideas
of supply, freedom, wholeness, and growth escape our
translating them into tangible blessings if we keep them
centered in our consciousness. And as we become consumed
by our own spiritual thinking, so we are raised in consciousness.

St. Francis of Assisi, hoeing his garden one day, was

supposed to have been asked what he would do if he were suddenly to learn that he was to die at sunset. He said, "I would finish hoeing my garden." He was not expressing fatalism or deceiving himself; rather he had attained serenity of spirit and found the way to step into eternity now. He knew the goodness of life wherever he was, in celestial objects, in nature, and wildlife. He had made his peace with the past, had no anxiety about the future, and knew everything in its entirety was here and now. He worked without striving, believed without probing, existed without having to question why. This is the description of a real saint, not just of St. Francis.

We only have to take one step at a time to succeed, to overcome, to demonstrate whatever we seek on the spiritual path. Time in this relative world tempts us into many sidetracks, but as Jesus told the prospective disciple, "No one who puts his hand to the plow and looks back is fit for the kingdom of God." His companion thought was taught to the multitude. "Therefore do not be anxious about tomorrow, for tomorrow will be anxious for itself."

After all, what can be more exciting than to step into eternity now!

YOUR TRUE IDENTITY

The identity of self, your soul, is your divine estate. It develops spiritually from the inspiration of God, but the outer impressions and experiences also contribute to its character of self. Although the metaphysical term consciousness is used often synonymous with the word soul, no other word can really match the excellence, dignity, and meaning of the word soul to better express the immortal you. The soul God breathed into being as you is your sacred possession of self. I believe Plato expressed this truth so clearly when he said, "Of all things which a man has . . . his soul is most truly his own."

The Greeks, who had a name for everything, used the term "psyche" for soul. Psyche means the breath of life, and also butterfly. The latter meaning is symbolic of the transcendent self rising up from mortality and human struggle to be resplendent and free as it travels through space, time, and circumstance on the spiritual path. The Unity emblem stands for the soul's right to spiritual ascendancy. It traces back to an ancient Egyptian symbol representing the relation between Spirit, soul, and body. Lowell Fillmore once explained the wings of Unity in these words: "As man develops spiritual consciousness, he attains the realization of the soul as the wings of the body. Back of the soul is Spirit, which quickens and energizes the soul; that is, gives the soul wings." So we can see that the soul is the entity of identity which survives the past, lives in the eternal now and embraces eternity. The Spirit of God is always giving life to the soul as the Psalmist affirmed, "'Wither shall I go from thy Spirit? Or whither shall I flee from thy presence?"

Modern psychiatry and psychology lose the spiritual depth of the word soul. Among reference books I have on the mental sciences I cannot find the term soul once in the index. Even so, those professions had to lean heavily upon the Greek term for the soul as is evident in their identification—psychiatry, psychology, psychoanalysis, psychometry, psychotherapy, and all the variations prefixed "psych." The clinical, professional terms lose the poetry, sense of inner self value, affection that is inspired by the word soul. Finally, all professional treatment fails if it does not reach where the Mighty Counselor can minister to His very own. Shakespeare made it so clear in phrasing the question in one of his plays, "Who is it that can tell me who I am?" This matter of terms and their application is not constant in our changing world and today there is great evidence that metaphysical and spiritual thought are making a contributing influence upon psychiatry. I see the higher approach in all professions merging them into a unity and breaking down the walls of blind specialization.

In many ways the soul must be felt deeply to be known. It must be exalted as the great value of self and held with reverence and respect as God's most supreme creation. As a child I was reminded repeatedly by my mother that soul was my spiritual self and she drummed integrity and high principles into my head with regard to every life encounter I faced in my growing years. Her favorite Bible verse, from the King James version, was quoted to me time and time again with a penetrating eye contact that reinforced her communication, "For what shall it profit a man, if he shall gain the whole world, and lose his own soul? or what shall a man give in exchange for his soul?" This went beyond moralizing, preaching, or even explaining. She got me to feel the value of my soul-nature and the equity in it I shared with God.

Edmond Sinnott, a leading biologist, was convinced the Spirit is ensouled in all nature. His conviction was that a rose blooms as a rose because the rose-identity is already established within. More and more our great scientists are testifying how all their research proves an organizational center is active to protect and perpetuate the idea of identity in all the natural phenomena they explore. Some have reported examples of how the creative identity continually unites to serve a higher unity. Emerson held the concept of the Over-Soul. Teilhard de Chardin in his masterful work *The Phenomenon of Man* speaks of an Omega point where there is an emersion of souls into a higher, heavenly unity. He said, "All around us, one by one, like a continual exhalation, 'souls' break away, carrying upwards their incommunicable load of consciousness. One by one, yet not in isolation." We gain so much understanding of creation when we see the value of the soul as it should be regarded in the relationship of all souls as the "Children of God." As we merge in love, understanding, tolerance, world brotherhood, the reconciliation of human differences, there unfolds a unity that reaches beyond our mortality.

In the human exchange of living so much is only expressed on a mundane verbal level. We have compounded knowledge, structured society to heights of sophistication, and explored the mind with great penetration. The soul is more than body, mind, and personality. The soul is the very seat of each individual's identity. Soul-to-soul communication required the development of loving perception and spiritual sensitivity. To really see a rose one must see the heart hidden in the bud and bloom. To see a sunrise one must also be aware that it portrays the wakeful eye of God greeting the observer of the dawn. The soul is the poetry of creation, the book of immortality, the scribe of the spirit, the home provided for you forever where one day you and God will always be perfectly at home together.

Reflecting on the question, "Who is it that can tell me who I am?"—cannot the Spirit of God that now breathes the very life that sustains your soul? Paul taught that spiritual things must be spiritually discerned . . . "We have received not the spirit of the world, but the Spirit which is from God, that we might understand the gifts bestowed on us by God." All the wisdom and truth of the ages, the purest teachings of the great religions, all our hungering and thirsting for righteousness, all are proclaiming "Be still, and know that I am God." Each time we return to the temple of self and truly find our soul identity, ego dissolves and personality steps aside. Self of self, Life of life, Light of light, Love of love, the Lord of one's being always assures the soul I Am and with My Power and My Presence you are. In the merging of the outer self with the Inner Self comes that individual consciousness called grace.

Today my mother's words still echo the unanswerable question of Jesus' words, "What shall a man give in exchange for his soul?" My only conclusion is that the soul is not exchangeable, only redeemable. And once one feels in possession of his soul nothing can make him feel insecure. William Ernest Henley, English poet and writer of the late 19th century suffered many tragic circumstances in his life, yet he resolutely thanked God for his "unconquerable soul." He closed his well-known poem "Invictus" with the words, "I am the master of my fate: I am the captain of my soul." It is in sensing the spiritual value of one's creation that we dispel the shadowy outer self with a light that lightens the world. Identification with God in you, in me, in every person as a child of God tells you who you are. When other terms of identity prove to be inadequate because they are stating only partial identity, think of yourself as a soul, a living soul quickened by the very Spirit of God.

If you believe the entity of self, your soul, is your

divine estate, invite the unity of your Christ Self and soul self to take place. Let yourself be one. The happening of this inner communion was beautifully described with a vision of excellence when John wrote his Revelation, "Behold, I stand at the door and knock; if anyone hears my voice and opens the door, I will come in to him and eat with him, and he with me. He who conquers I will grant him to sit with me on my throne, as I myself conquered and sat down with my Father on his throne."

TRUST AND REST

God speaks to us in many ways—
Sometimes in things we call delays.
How always final outcomes show
That higher truth we have to know!
We must use time to trust and rest
And let God's way prove what is
best.

GOD SHAPES ME

I am more than matter, form and flesh,
*   More than this intricate human mesh.*
I am the essence that whispers "Me" —
*   God shapes my identity!*

MY OWN HEART SONG

The ringing of a bell sets free
A deep imprisoned melody,
An echoing that loudly rings
And like a bird takes off on wings
Until its distant pealing sound
No longer to the shell is bound.

And I, God's instrument, do long
To echo forth my own heart song;
For like the hollowed bell that
      rings,
My heart is empty till it sings—
Sings out with soulful joy sublime,
Trancending earth, self, space,
      and time!

MEDITATION

I have eternal time at my command. Every moment is precious to me in my becomingness. The Divine "I" is forever lifting my consciousness to a more glorified expression. I stand somewhere between Alpha and Omega. The best is yet to be! As I learn to enjoy the divinity within my humanness, I find the secret of true happiness and "let patience have her perfect work." In contentment my soul cannot be hurried or pressured. I will not be anxious.

Although I have not seen the whole light, I know the beauty and wonder of its spectrum. My focus on eternity is improving. My appreciation for why all this must be is enhanced in every daily rebirth. The original creation waits for my spirituality to be complete, for my coming of age; then I shall take my rightful place with the elders of the higher dimensions. Whichever of the many mansions I may enter, I will be at home in my Father's house.

Time unfolds quickly enough for me in the eternal now. It brings perpetual opportunity. As quickly as I release the past the present frees me to create a better future. I am a sojourner, a traveler in space and time. I am a citizen of the universe. Whoever shares the same path with me becomes my divine companion. Whatever happens to me will serve my higher good, not in the finite sense but in terms of my letting all things work together for good. Insight after insight, Truth reveals Itself and I become more illumined. In my incompleteness I see myself wonderfully made. My destiny is divine. In the perfection of my soul my Creator is exalted. "Glorify thy Son that the Son may glorify thee."

AFFIRMATION LEADS TO REALIZATION

An affirmation is a statement of truth declared silently or audibly to unify one's consciousness. It is not the spiritual answer, but a way to initiate realization. Mentally, a positive affirmation spoken with faith can have a dynamic effect. All positive thinking is a thought-conditioning method good as far as it goes. Spiritually, affirmation should initiate a higher level of awareness that can sustain itself without a person having to be continually assertive. Contrary to what many teachers often suggest, affirmations should not be said over and over again. Jesus termed this kind of mental merry-go-round thinking "vain repetition."

Think of an affirmation as being like the prelude to a symphony of the soul. It can begin the sweet accord for the whole orchestration of spiritual faculties to assemble and play their divine part. The conscious declaration of truth helps you awaken to the inner mind, make your entry to the domain of the Divine "I." It is as Jesus taught, "I am the vine, you are the branches. He who abides in me, and I in him, he it is that bears much fruit, for apart from me you can do nothing." Affirmation, then, is the booster thought from the mental plane to reach a state of spiritual realization.

Because I have never met anyone who was beyond needing a good affirmation now and then, the following may serve as a guide for the reader. Affirmations can merely be positive thinking of a motivational nature, but I prefer the employment of affirmation all the way with the goal of self-realization. Administer the spiritual idea to yourself for a personal need, but go beyond the personal concern to the experience of meditation. Learn to enjoy the ease of spirit that is not dependent upon mind techniques or metaphysical methods. When the positive mind yields to spiritual awareness true realization occurs. The main thing is to speak the word of Truth for yourself in a quiet posture of mind, centering your inner forces and accepting the simple premise that God is the answer to every need. "You will decide on a matter, and it will be established for you, and light will shine on your ways." (Job 22:2)

SPIRITUAL SELF-AWARENESS — I AM THE INDIVID-UATED EXPRESSION OF GOD AS A LIVING SOUL. MY TRUE SELF IS GOD-SELF.
"I am the way, and the truth, and the life." (John 14:6)
"He who is in you is greater than he who is in the world." (I John 4:4)

UNDERSTANDING — ALL TRUTH IS SELF-REVEAL-ING AND I AM FOREVER ALERT AND RECEPTIVE TO ITS DIVINE INSTRUCTION.
"It is the spirit in a man, the breath of the Almighty, that makes him understand." (Job 32:8)
"When the Spirit of truth comes, he will guide you into all the truth." (John 16:13)

PEACE OF MIND — I RELEASE ANXIOUS THOUGHT, ACCEPT SPIRIT'S WAY OF EASE, AND DIVINE CON-TENTMENT IS NOW MINE.
"Thou dost keep him in perfect peace, whose mind is stayed on thee, because he trusts in thee." (Isaiah 26:3)
"Peace I leave with you; my peace I give to you; not as the world gives do I give to you. Let not your hearts be troubled, neither let them be afraid." (John 14:27)

ORDER — I LET THE PRINCIPLE OF UNIVERSAL ORDER GOVERN MY MIND, BODY AND AFFAIRS. MY LIFE IS DIVINELY ADJUSTED DAY BY DAY.
"Do not be conformed to this world but be transformed by the renewal of your mind, that you may prove what is the will of God, what is good and acceptable and perfect." (Romans 12:2)

GUIDANCE — THE ALL-KNOWING MIND ILLUMINES MY MIND AND MAKES CLEAR MY WAY. I AM DIVINELY GUIDED.
"The word is a lamp to my feet and a light to my path." (Psalms 119:105)
"In all your ways acknowledge him, and he will make straight your paths." (Proverbs 3:6)

HUMAN RELATIONS — I BEHOLD CHRIST IN EVERYONE. I GIVE PERSONALITY NO POWER AND IT HAS NO POWER OVER ME.
"Christ is all, and in all." (Colossians 3:11)
"This is my commandment, that you love one another as I have loved you." (John 15:12)

HEALING — PERFECT SPIRIT GENERATES PERFECT LIFE IN ME. MY FAITH SEES ONLY THE WHOLENESS AND I HOLD MY LIFE IMAGE SACRED.
"Pleasant words are like a honeycomb, sweetness to the soul and health to the body." (Proverbs 16:24)
"Your eye is the lamp of your body; when your eye is sound, your whole body is full of light." (Luke 11:34)

FORGIVENESS — I FORGIVE WITHOUT EFFORT BECAUSE I DO NOT JUDGE.
"Judge not that you be not judged." (Matt. 7:1)
"Beloved, if our hearts do not condemn us, we have confidence before God." (I John 3:21)

LOVE – DIVINE LOVE EXPRESSING THROUGH ME IS THE HEALING, HARMONIZING, QUICKENING POWER IN MY LIFE AND AFFAIRS. ALL WHO FEEL ITS TOUCH AND KNOW ITS PULSE ARE ONE WITH ME.
"He who does not love does not know God; for God is love." (I John 4:8)
"Love bears all things, believes all things, hopes all things, endures all things." (I Corinthians 13:7)

PROSPERITY – INFINITE POWER, IDEAS AND SUB-STANCE FLOW THROUGH MY SOUL AND SUPPLY MY EVERY NEED. MY FAITH AND EXPECTATION ATTRACT WHAT IS RIGHTFULLY MINE AND FOR MY HIGHEST GOOD.
"All that the Father has is mine." (John 16:15)
"The Lord is my shepherd, I shall not want." (Psalms 23:1)

SUCCESS – GOD IN ME CANNOT FAIL. WITH TIRE-LESS EFFORT, ETERNAL TRUST, AND A CONFI-DENT SPIRIT I OVERCOME OUTER LIMITATION.
"I can do all things in him who strengthens me." (Philippians 4:13)
"I tell you, lift up your eyes, and see how the fields are already white for harvest." (John 4:35)

BIBLIOGRAPHY

Science of Mind magazine (Permission to reprint gratefully acknowledged)

"Be Master of the Moment" — November 1958
"Relax and Live" — October 1969
"Communication Gap" — October 1971
"The Eternity Factor" — August 1977

Daily Word

"Love's Countenance" — November 1958
"You Can Be Free" — July 1959
"The Magic Touch" — October 1970
"Miracle Called Spring" — April 1977
"My Own Heart Song" — November 1978

Unity Magazine

"When I Am Still" — December 1958
"Take A Healing Walk" — March 1967
"Your Inner Gyroscope" — February 1969
"Consciousness Communicates" — May 1969
"The Power of a Fraction" — June 1969
"The Dynamics of Affirmation" — August 1969
"The Door Swings Both Ways" — October 1969
"Seeing Life in Its True Light" — January 1970
"Atoms and Stars" — July 1970
"The Creative Void" — September 1970
"The Gospel Truth" — March 1971

"The True Yoga" — September 1971
"From Karma to Grace" — October 1971
"The World is Going Metaphysical" — October 1972
"Programmed for Perfection" — November 1974
"The Tendrils of Life" — June 1975
"The Alchemy of Thought" — February 1976
"The Next Larger Context" — July 1976
"Idea Power" — November 1976
"The Metaphysical Trinity" — May 1977
"A Little Gift For You" — December 1977
"Such As I Have" — May 1978
"The Mind Lock" — October 1978
"The Quiet Way Will Overcome" — March 1979

Weekly Unity

"God Reflected in a Sparrow's Eye" — July 21, 1968
"You Know You Can Do It" — October 12, 1969
"Bless and be Blessed" — October 25, 1970
"Trust and Rest" — November 1, 1970
"Empathy" — February 7, 1971
"Not Without Love" — July 4, 1971

Good Business

"Time is Our Responsibility" — January 1957
"It's Your Move" — March 1957

Truth Journal

"Your True Identity" — March 1975
"All the Time You Need" — March 1977